Securing Your Wealth

A Complete Guide to Retirement Investing

Marcus Papajohn, CFS, CSA

Contents

Preface

Throughout the years I have seen many expensive investing and asset management mistakes. Smart, knowledgeable people make errors in their finances that cost thousands and hundreds of thousands of dollars in lost principal and lost opportunity. These simple errors often include but are not limited to the following:

- Needlessly paying taxes on social security income

- Paying excessive taxes on mutual fund holdings

- Naming the wrong beneficiary on an IRA

- Leaving double-taxed assets in the estate

I wrote this book to help investors avoid these and many other common financial mistakes. We are in an age of do-it-yourself. An investor can make their own investments and find useful information in self-help magazines, on-line services, Internet sites, investment newsletters, etc. There is no shortage of financial tips and strategies. Even with all of these resources at their fingertips, many investors still feel starved for the right information.

The aforementioned sources can explain thousands of different investment options and financial techniques. They can show you literally millions of ways to put together your own portfolio and manage your assets; however, none of these sources will directly address your personal circumstances. That's where a financial advisor comes in. I am certainly biased because I advise people about their finances for a living, but I must share with you, most people could save a great deal more just by avoiding common mistakes.

Many people do not realize that once they reach age 55, there can be a shift in their investment goals. It may no longer be all about making as much money as possible, but about protecting what they have worked their entire lives for: their home, their investments, and their family.

*This book is devoted to my clients
who have placed their trust in me
and have realized the financial fruits
of a great working relationship.*

Chapter One

Retirement Planning

Retirement planning is quite simply the practice of determining what you want to accomplish with your money so you're not caught off guard when things change. On any given day, you can pick up the newspaper and see ads for the "greatest" mutual fund or "greatest" annuity or you can get a "hot tip" down at the coffee shop. The only way to defend yourself from all of this noise is to have a plan for what you want to accomplish. With a plan in place you won't need to react to every new idea that comes along.

Different investors have different goals. Investors may be concerned that they do not have sufficient assets to meet their needs and are nervous that if it's a concern today, will they have enough in the future when they need even more? Will it last? What if they run out? They may be frustrated about the amount of money they are losing in taxes, worried that paying the taxes today may mean less money is available for themselves or their families in the future. Often, investors are upset because their investments are down a significant amount and they're concerned that they may not have enough time or the right investments to get back their original principal, let alone make a profit. And, over the last few years retirees have become increasingly anxious about the rising costs of nursing care and their ability to pay for it without putting their home, their investments and their family at risk.

Determining your primary goals is the first step in creating a financial plan that will help to address your problems and put you on the right path. It is helpful to be aware of some of the most common mistakes made by investors.

AVOID THREE COMMON INVESTMENT MISTAKES

Making money is primarily about protecting against loss. If you are able avoid investment "mistakes", the profits will tend to take care of themselves. It is important to note that you need a 43% gain to recover from a 30% loss on your investment. Many investors are putting themselves in a position where they must earn a 43% gain on their investments just to maintain their same standard of living. The avoidance of losses can be much more important than the acquisition of profits. No investment system can guarantee profits, but by avoiding these 3 common investment mistakes you can certainly increase your odds:

1. **Try not to pay attention to investment forecasts or the current state of the economy.** The newspaper journalists, radio and television talk show hosts, and financial magazines all tell you how to invest based on what will happen in the future. These "experts" are taking an educated guess at best. They have no more an idea about what the future has in store than any other human being.

The world is in constant flux and you should attempt to ignore these occurrences when making investment decisions. Look at some of the events of the 90s:

▪ Many investors cashed in their stocks when Saddam Hussein invaded Kuwait. They sold their stocks at the bottom (Dow Jones Average 2350) out of panic. Four months later Hussein was sent back home and what appeared to be a major world event became a memory. The market quickly recovered and set off on one of the greatest bull markets in history.

▪ In the fall of 1998, with the Dow Jones Industrial Average trading around 8000, some investors concerned that the depression in Asia would spread worldwide, moved their growth investments to cash. Asia is now on the road to recovery and those investors have missed a very nice run of appreciation in US stocks.

There will always be another "tragedy," and I recommend you forget about the economic news and other world events when making investment decisions because they change too quickly. As soon as the media determines that "utilities look good" or "now's the time to buy bonds," it is already too late.

Your own needs are the most important indicator of how you should be investing. Your needs change very slowly over time and may not change at all once you retire. If you allow your needs to be your guide and forget about the external environment you will invest accordingly and stop worrying about the future. You can not control what the future holds, but you can control what you do in the present.

2. **You must prepare for inflation.** While you're working inflation is not much of a factor. You receive increases in your pay to offset the rising costs of goods and services. Once in retirement, even a 3% annual rate of inflation could slowly erode your standard of living.

In order to outpace inflation, some of your money should always be in growth investments such as stocks, mutual funds, or real estate. If you ignore inflation, you could have retirement that becomes increasingly more uncomfortable with age.

3. **Do your estate planning immediately.** Far too many families experience lengthy, costly probate estate settlements. Billions in estate taxes each year are paid to the IRS that could have been avoided. Estate planning is not as difficult as many make it out to be. The cost of procrastination can be severe for those you care about most; your family.

There are no "quick fix" solutions to bettering your standard of living and what you do today will impact you for years to come.

THE DIFFERENCE BETWEEN RICH AND POOR

The words of my college sociology professor remain lodged in my head. "One of the primary differences between rich people and poor people," he explained, "is that rich people have longer time horizons." The wealthy tend to think and plan long-term. He went on to say that often "when poor people have money, they will look to spend their money right away," insisting that "a poor person who wins the lottery will often spend the total of their winnings within a year, in some cases incurring large debts."

"Rich people" he said, "will tend to invest for the future. The wealthy typically have a longer time horizon and are unaffected by the "catastrophe du jour; the Russian financial collapse, domestic recession, the invasion of Kuwait, currency devaluation, real estate meltdown, tax law changes, or presidential impeachment." Rich investors think in five and ten year increments and invest accordingly. Many investors would be well served to adopt such a methodology in their own investing. Long-term investors have the ability to buy low (when everyone else is frantic) and sell high (when everyone else is frantic).

Everyone understands the concept of "buy low and sell high" but most investors don't do it. The problem is emotion. It is difficult to invest when the news is bad, and that is exactly when many wealthy investors have created their fortunes.

As the very wealthy investor John Templeton professed, "The best places to invest are those areas of greatest pessimism. Some investors will shy away from these places, others will reap tremendous rewards."

SOME RETIREES DIGGING FINANCIAL GRAVE

"Conventional wisdom" may be the most dangerous guide to your financial management. Conventional wisdom is something that is believed by everyone to be true. In fact, it is believed so completely that it is rarely challenged. However, when scrutinized this wisdom has often failed to be entirely accurate:

- Bonds are more conservative than stocks

- The higher the risk, the higher the return

- The stock market does best when we have a Republican president

The majority of investors think bonds will make their portfolio more conservative when in fact they may be making their portfolio much more risky.

Summary of an article that appeared in the AAII Journal, in February, 1998

At some point in time, every retiree faces the problem of determining how much to keep in the stock market vs. how much to keep in bonds. Many investors mistakenly believe that keeping more money in bonds produces a safer portfolio and greater financial security. Based on the study by AAII, this conclusion is incorrect.

Hypothetical Example:

Mr. Smith, a retiree, uses his $500,000 portfolio to generate $40,000 per year of income. Measuring since the end of WWII, if that portfolio were invested 50% in stocks and 50% in high grade corporate bonds there is only a 48% chance that the portfolio would have lasted. However, if that portfolio were invested 100% in stocks, there is a 90% chance that the portfolio would have made it.

The study concluded that stocks have been a far safer alternative in the post war period for making retiree assets last. However, because bonds fluctuate less, most people continue to think bonds are a safer investment. Apparently, the greater fluctuation of stocks in the short-term does not make them less safe over the long-term. It is by focusing on the short run that some investors draw conclusions which are incorrect, and possibly devastating to their long-term financial well-being.

The appropriate allocation of stocks and bonds depends on the degree to which you rely on your portfolio for current income and how comfortable you are with fluctuations in the short run. Determining the right investment can be difficult, especially in the face of conventional wisdom.

INTELLECTUALS MAY HAVE MORE TROUBLE MANAGING THEIR INVESTMENTS

I met a very bright man a while back, a retired engineer for a well-known global engineering company. During his career, he had worked on many extremely difficult and mentally challenging projects, but when it came to his investments, his portfolio had declined in value since retiring, even during times the market had been soaring. How could such a smart professional do so poorly in his own personal investing?

There is little to no correlation between intelligence and investment results. In fact, intellectual people will frequently study and take in far too much information to be able to make sound investment decisions. The result can be procrastination and indecision.

One of the problems with the information investors receive is that it is often conflicting *opinions*. One "expert" may say one thing, while another "expert" will most certainly say another. The investor who listens to these opinions is often confused, and can make bad investment decisions because of it.

The *stock market does not follow human logic.* A logical person with some knowledge of financial markets knows that the stock market suffered one of the worst bear markets in history between 2000 and 2002. Yet, in 2003 the stock market was up 22%. Investors who steered clear of stocks in 2003 missed huge gains to their portfolio.

Making a poor investment decision can be frustrating and emotionally very difficult. A failed investment however, does not mean that you are in some way lacking intelligence. Nor does your membership in the Mensa round table society make you an investment guru. A sound investment strategy that is not overly complex is the key to a successful retirement

KNOWING ABOUT THIS SEESAW COULD
SAVE YOU BIG MONEY

When "experts" discuss the stock market they often divide stocks into industry categories such as industrial, utility, financial, electronic, etc... A simple categorization of stocks into two types; value and growth, can be extremely helpful in protecting capital.

Growth stocks are stocks of companies with rapid growth potential (15% a year or more expected growth in earnings). These stocks are typically well regarded in the marketplace, get lots of press, and trade at expensive price to earnings multiples: Intel, Dell, Microsoft, etc... Growth stocks do best during "hot" markets. However, during periods of market decline, growth stocks will often lose the most. In fact, it's not uncommon in a down market or after a disappointing earnings report to see a "hot" growth stock lose 50% of its value in as short a period as 2 weeks.

Value stocks are typically less well regarded in the marketplace. They have slower growth prospects and are not as "sexy" or "popular": General Motors, Du Pont, etc... They typically do not advance as rapidly during "hot" markets as do growth stocks, however, during down markets, value stocks tend to hold their value better than their often overpriced counterpart. Because value stocks are not as talked about, an excited public has not inflated their prices.

Many investors will want to take a more defensive position during periods when they think the market is about to decline by switching out of growth stocks into value stocks. It is important to remember that it is impossible to predict market direction with any degree of accuracy. Peter Lynch says he can't do it, Warren Buffet says he won't attempt it and John Templeton reports that he ignores market direction all together.[1]

LESSONS FROM WARREN BUFFET

If you don't already know, Warren Buffet is one of the most successful investors of our generation. He accumulated over $30 billion of personal wealth by investing in the stock market. Notice I did not say he accumulated his wealth "by trading stocks." In fact, 96% of market returns have nothing to do with stock picking or market timing. Warren Buffet knows this. It might be wise to pattern your investing after the major principals he uses. Below are some direct quotes and summaries of his philosophy that demonstrate what Warren Buffet thinks as opposed to what many investors think:

Buffet: Trying to predict market swings is unimportant.
Investors: What effect will rising interest rates have on my stocks?

Buffet: A short focus is not conducive to profits, you need to be patient.
Investors: Should I buy internet stocks now?

Buffet: There seems to be some perverse human characteristic that likes to make easy things difficult.
Investors: I heard on CNBC this morning that utility companies will probably cut their dividends so doesn't that mean I should....?

Buffet: The most important quality for an investor is temperament, not intellect.
Investors: I watch the Nightly Business Report so that I can learn as much as possible about investing.

As Buffet would be the first to tell you not to attempt to predict the stock market he might also note that past performance is not indicative of future performance.

DON'T BECOME A VICTIM OF THE
LOTTERY TICKET EFFECT

A number of investors are currently watching a stock they purchased years ago at a premium fall into the single digit range. Maybe they are thinking, "It was over $150 three years ago. I can get it at a bargain for $4 today, and if it goes up to even ½ of where it was before, I'll be looking good." Just like buying a lottery ticket with the hope of winning that $100 million jackpot, the odds are not in your favor.

In the past, stocks that have gone below $5 seldom recover. Those that tumble beneath a dollar generally get delisted by NASDAQ, must trade over-the-counter, and rarely make a comeback. Quite often these low-priced securities become the subject of hours of discussion in Internet chat rooms. I have even heard of situations where these stocks are pushed by high-pressure brokers who are trying to pump up the profits of their own stocks.

There is no shortage of low-priced stocks to choose from. The percentage of NASDAQ stocks trading for less than $5 has gone from 20% in March of 2000, to 46% by the third quarter of 2002. In March of 2000 only 28 companies traded for less than $1, while 550 had fallen that far by August of 2002.

Stocks that trade for less than $5 are two to three times more volatile (risky) than stocks that sell for more than $25. Those stocks that sell for between $5 and $10 are 50% more erratic. Needless to say, low-priced stocks are very unstable and for good reason. Mutual funds and pensions, the leading long-term owners of equities, seldom buy stocks that sell for less than $5. Additionally, the spreads between the bid and the ask price tends to increase when the stock price is low, adding to the volatility.

Hypothetical Example:

The difference between the bid and the ask prices on a $5 stock are 3%. This means that the price could go up or down by that amount after one trade. In contrast, if an investor bought 100 shares of a $50 stock and paid $50 in commission, the price fluctuation would only be 1%.

If you find yourself tempted to buy so-called "bargain stocks," keep in mind that the low price alone is not enough of a reason to invest in a company. You can be sure that the price is low for a good reason.

SENIORS AND FINANCIAL CHALLENGES

I meet a lot of retirees with sizeable estates whose spouse is no longer alive. Often the surviving spouse is left to address issues that heretofore had been "taken care of" by their now deceased wife or husband. Confused about what actions they should be taking to preserve their financial security and that of their heirs, many will do nothing at all. Below are some ideas that can provide some direction.

Inaction can be just as bad as incorrect action. We often think that we can only make a mistake by acting. However, failure to take action can be just as costly. Look at what happens when we don't change the oil in our cars. The engine can seize up, resulting in a $5,000 engine rebuild cost. Doing nothing should not be considered a safe solution. The markets, taxes and changing legislation can erode the value of an estate while the owner does nothing.

Financial matters don't have to be confusing. Do not deal with anyone who makes financial matters complicated or uses jargon. If you cannot follow 100% of what he or she explains or advises, then switch to another advisor. Such issues are confusing only when you select someone who is a poor teacher or guide.

Make sure that you have adequate income for your personal needs. You need to write down your monthly expenses. With a totaled list, you can then determine how much of your investments are required for income. The remaining investments can be allocated for growth in your estate.

Confide in someone and show them your total situation. Show a qualified advisor all of your investment statements, bank accounts and insurance policies. With the whole picture in plain view, you can start to get appropriate advice.

These simple steps can lead to a more certain and peaceful existence. Don't let the passing of your spouse leave you feeling all alone.

IS YOUR FINANCIAL ADVISOR ANY GOOD?

It seemed like anyone could pick a winning portfolio in the late 1990s. Many so called investment professionals seemed to think the Bull-run would last forever. But, the bubble burst. It was only in the beginning of 2000 that many financial advisors began to show their true colors. Often when investors see their returns decline they start to question their relationship with their current financial advisor. They feel unimportant and ignored and get the feeling that it is time to make a change. The following four questions will help you determine if your financial advisor has your best interests in mind:

1. **Who benefits more from your investments, you or your financial advisor?**
   Most people go to a stock broker or advisor to get some independent advice. Many advisors push investments managed by their firm known as "proprietary products." These investments often deliver the most profit to their firm and their firm's advisors.

   Hypothetical Example:

   Your advisor represents XYZ Securities. The vast majority of the investments in your portfolio include the name XYZ Securities (i.e. XYZ Growth & Income Fund). This does not necessarily mean that this is a poor investment. To ensure the quality of your investments, it is a good idea to compare them to other like investments. You need to know if the investments in your portfolio were recommended because they are good for you and your situation and not simply because it's good for your advisor's firm.

2. **Does your advisor do all the talking?**
   Your advisor must be knowledgeable about all aspects of your financial life. Too often financial advisors do not account for the whole picture and wind up making recommendations that are not appropriate for your overall situation. You may want to ask yourself the following questions of your advisor:

- Has he or she ever asked to see your tax return? Failure to understand your tax situation may result in a loss of thousands of dollars.

- Is he or she willing and able to answer questions that you have relating to estate planning?

- Does he or she get back to you in a timely manner?

3. **Do you like what you own?**
Your advisor must take into account your feelings, goals and concerns when making a recommendation. You should understand your investment portfolio and never feel like your advisor is pushing items on you that you don't comprehend. If your investments cause you to worry day after day, then the items in your portfolio may not accurately represent you as an investor. A good advisor must consider your comfort level when making any investment recommendations. If you're losing sleep over your investment performance, then your investments may not be right for you.

4. **Does your advisor buy and sell and buy and sell and buy and ....**
Market timing and picking the right security account for less than 4% of overall account performance. The number of transactions in your account is representative of the type of investor you are. The more your account buys and sells, the more aggressive you are as an investor. Take your most recent account statement and compare the items in your portfolio today versus the items in your portfolio one year ago. If you are a conservative investor, only 30% or 40% of your portfolio should turnover every year. A high

rate of turnover may mean more short-term gains, and short-term gains are taxed at the highest rates.

While the list of questions may be much more extensive, you should always address these issues before selecting a financial advisor. An additional, but important item that is often overlooked is how your financial advisor is compensated.

GOOD ADVICE ISN'T FREE

In the past it didn't matter whether you were dealing with a stockbroker, an account executive, or a financial planner. You paid a commission every time they made a transaction. The goal was to get some good advice before making any sort of change. Until recently this was the only option on paying for financial advice.

A new fee arrangement has come into play, in which the advisor is not compensated in the form of a commission for transacting business. The fee-based advisor charges a yearly fee for managing your portfolio or an hourly fee for advice.

The advisors who charge fees will say that the commission advisors have an incentive for you to buy and sell in order to generate a commission. An advisor would be reluctant to promote a buy and hold strategy if they were not commissioned to do so. The Advisors who charge commissions question paying an ongoing fee if your portfolio remains unchanged for long periods of time. I would argue that the question of how you pay an advisor is far less important than other criteria:

- Trusting the Advisor and their abilities,

- Receiving advice consistent with your goals and objectives,

- Having your investments consistently perform in the top quartile of its peers.

When you work with an advisor you trust, how you pay them is a matter of personal preference. Both the commission-based and fee-based advisor can obtain and recommend similar investments to you. What is important is that they are recommending the best investments for your situation.

WHY DO I NEED A FINANCIAL ADVISOR?

Unfortunately, investors are often their own worst enemy. Many investors get off track because they invest based on what they read in the newspaper, hear on the radio, or see on the television. Many people invest emotionally, believing that there is a direct correlation between a stock's performance and the current news. This correlation is weak and may cause you to make mistakes. The news will cause you to make inappropriate investment decisions for a number of reasons:

1. **The news released to the public is late, often reflecting what has already happened.** For example, weeks before the State tobacco settlement was reached, people who understood the law and the issue already saw what the settlement would mean to Philip Morris. This information was then disseminated to the "smart money." Weeks later, when the settlement was announced to the Press and published for the public, it was already old news.

2. **The news is already "discounted" (included) in the price of stocks.** Years ago, many investors thought that the stock market would fall because of problems in Asia. Because everyone knew about the problems in Asia, stock prices already reflected this bad news. The stock market does not react to the news, but rather it precedes it. In fact, the next time people start saying the stock market will fall, it is probably a pretty good time to buy because the prices will already have been driven down.

3. **What you read in the press reflects only the variables that the press can take the time to understand and analyze.** There are dozens of important variables that impact the price of a stock. Journalists are not financial experts. Due to understanding and time constraints, they report only the simpler issues. Sometimes the truly important factors that push a stock price up or down are missed.

A study by Terrance Odean of the University of California at Davis analyzed the daily trading records and monthly positions of 88,000 investors at a large discount brokerage firm. The data covers a span of 10 years and looks at over 2 million common stock trades. The study concluded that investors trade too actively, are under diversified, cling to losers, and buy stocks that happen to grab their attention. Many investors were found to have been motivated by overconfidence, the desire to avoid regret, and the difficulty of evaluating thousands of investment alternatives.

Remember, this was a study of people who wanted to invest on their own through discount brokerage accounts. The study found that the surer an investor was, the worse they would do. The 20% of investors who traded most earned an average net annual return *5.5% lower* than that of the least active traders in the study.

The hallmark of a truly experienced, sophisticated investor is that they realize;

- They cannot consider all of the investment possibilities

- They are influenced by the news

- They are overconfident (a common American trait proven in several studies)

- They will not take a loss when they should.

As a result of knowing themselves, wise investors hire professionals to manage their financial planning needs. A financial professional cannot guarantee superior investment performance, but they can assist you in creating a strategy that is appropriate for your needs and goals. It's not about hitting a home run every time; it's about finishing the game.

AVOIDING PROBLEMS WITH YOUR FINANCIAL ADVISOR

We have all heard stories in the news of some "crooked" investment professional that stole someone's retirement plan and left the country. No matter how infrequent these scenarios, they will always exist. There is no way to guarantee that you won't get stuck with one of these "bad apples," but there are warning signs:

1.   **Never make a check directly payable to the advisor for any form of investment.** Instead, you should make the check payable to an investment firm that is not owned by the advisor. The only exception to this rule is for the payment of any consultation fees. Otherwise, this should send up a red flag.

2.   **Never invest in an investment that is controlled by the advisor.** If the advisor is putting together a few investors to buy an apartment building and the advisor is the general partner, he has total control over your funds.

3.   **Never invest in an illiquid investment.** Stocks, bonds, mutual funds and annuities are liquid. You can get out of them anytime. Exotic investments which promise high returns, such as oil and gas deals and equipment leasing deals are illiquid. You cannot get out. If something goes wrong with the investment, you could lose everything.

I do not mean to imply that by committing one of the above three actions that you will have a problem. However, when I do see problems, one or more of these three actions was typically involved.

Chapter Two

Income Investing

Most seniors depend on income from their investments. It is for this reason that they are more affected by declining interest rates than any other group. For countless retirees, CDs and treasury securities are the investments of choice. With rates now the lowest in more than 20 years, if investors keep depending on these sources, they may continue to find their income declining. This could lead to personal financial disaster. Living expenses will continue to increase while income steadily declines.

WHERE TO OBTAIN HIGHER PAYING CDs

Some banks do not have the expense of operating local branches and paying the salaries of tellers and new accounts people. By saving this money, they can pay you more interest. These banks are FDIC insured, just like your local bank. Shop around for the best Certificates of Deposit. Check out other banks and saving institutions in your neighborhood and in other states. Their rates are often higher than you can get locally. In fact, these rates are often 25% higher than the national averages.[2] You receive interest every month or calendar quarter, depending on your desires and your deposit is returned at maturity.

CALLABLE CDs

"Callable CDs" are a variety of CD that typically pays more than regular (non-callable) CDs. The FDIC insurance, full principal repayment at maturity and above-average yields appeals to safety conscious retirees looking for income.[3] Although FDIC insured, they have features that must be understood. Before you jump at the rate offered by some ad in the Sunday newspaper, you need to understand the features of callable CDs and how they work:

High Rate - The high rate could be temporary. Most callable CDs are callable after a year or two, which means, you could get paid off and your high rate would stop. Of course, you do not risk any principal, but you may need to find another place to invest, possibly at a lower rate. Banks offer callable CDs to shift interest-rate risk to the depositor. A callable CD will have a higher yield than a CD without a call provision because the depositor is taking on this interest-rate risk.[4] They may have terms of 10 or 20 years. These CDs are good for someone who does not need the liquidity, but would like the higher rates and safety of principal. Callable CDs are appropriate in a number of situations:

- Investors looking to protect the principal of money they don't need

- People who want to leave money for their heirs

- Those who need to safely maximize income

- Investors who have adequate liquid resources

Take these precautions – The only obligation the bank has is to pay you back at maturity. Most banks will buy back the CD from you sooner, but it could be at a steep discount. In the event of your death, some callable CDs may not allow your heirs to redeem the CDs until they have reached maturity. It is dependent upon the bank having enough funds in their "put" pool. Your heirs will have priority but could wait to see their money.

INDEX-LINKED CDs

Such CDs pay interest based on stock market performance, while protecting your principal from any downside. Your deposit is FDIC insured up to current limits.

Hypothetical Illustration:

Mr. Jones makes a deposit of $10,000 into an index linked CD. The CD has a 7.5 year maturity and is non-callable for 2 years. At the end of 7.5 years, he will receive his deposit back plus interest equal to the gain in the S&P 500 Index. Assume that the index increased 60% over the 7.5 years for a compound rate of 8%. He would receive $16,500.[5] However, if the stock market falls during the term of his CD his rate of return would be zero. Mr. Jones would receive his full deposit no matter what happens. The only way he could receive less than 100% of his original investment would be if he withdrew the principal prior to maturity. Some index-linked CDs may have additional features that you should understand:

Cap rate – The "cap rate" limits the gain by a percentage of the original amount invested. For example, a 100% cap rate would mean that a $10,000 CD would return no more than $20,000 no matter how high the index rose.

Call feature – This feature allows the issuing bank to redeem the CD before maturity at a pre-stated price.

Participation rate – The "participation rate" is the maximum percentage of the S&P index gains that you can receive. A 50% participation rate would enable the investor to enjoy half of the gains of the index (i.e. 3% of a 6% gain in the S&P).

If you think that the stock market performs well over the long term, index-linked CDs could interest you. It's an opportunity to participate in market gains without risk to principal.

UNDERSTANDING FDIC INSURANCE

Most people realize that their bank deposits are insured up to $100,000 per person, per institution. To ensure that all of your accounts are fully insured, you could just spread your money among different banks. However, you can also keep accounts at the same banks and get several hundred thousands of dollars of insurance if your accounts are organized correctly. The key is to use trusts or "pay-on-death" designations. Accounts that have named beneficiaries are insured $100,000 per named beneficiary.

*How a husband, wife and one child may have insured
amounts totaling $1,200,000*

Individual Account:	
Husband	$100,000
Wife	$100,000
Child	$100,000
Joint Accounts:	
Husband and Wife	$100,000
Husband and Child	$100,000
Wife and Child	$100,000
Revocable Trusts:	
Husband as a Trustee for Wife	$100,000
Husband as a Trustee for Child	$100,000
Wife as a Trustee for Husband	$100,000
Wife as a Trustee for Child	$100,000
Child as a Trustee for Father	$100,000
Child as a Trustee for Mother	$100,000
	$1,200,000

How Bonds Work

From providing additional income to diversifying your portfolio, investors use bonds to satisfy a variety of investment needs. But do you know what you are buying when you purchase a bond or a bond mutual fund?

Governments and corporations must raise money to expand or finance projects. These organizations sell bonds as a method of borrowing money. When you invest in a bond, you are lending money to its issuer. The bond is issued for a fixed period of time that can range from 13 weeks to 30 years. The issuer will make fixed-interest payments to the bond holder over the life of the bond and will pay them the face value of the bond when it matures.

There are several types of bonds on the market, the most common of which are:

- ***U.S. Treasury bonds*** - The federal government sells bonds to finance its debt. These bond issues are backed by the "full faith and credit" of the U.S. government. U.S. Treasury bonds are regarded as the most conservative investments available. Interest received is free from tax at the state level but is subject to federal income tax.

- ***Municipal bonds*** - State and local governments may use these funds to facilitate paying for the construction of schools and roads, as well as for land conservation. The interest from municipal bonds is usually exempt from federal and state income tax.

- ***GSE*** - Government-sponsored enterprise securities are sold by government agencies like Fannie Mae, Freddie Mac, and Ginnie Mae. This money is used to fund loans for special borrowers such as farmers, homebuyers, and students.

- ***Corporate bonds*** - Companies often need money to build or improve facilities, pay off old debt, to acquire other firms, or for expansion purposes. Interest from corporate bonds is taxable at the state and federal levels. Because corporate bonds are not backed by the "full faith and credit" of the government, they will often pay higher interest rates than government bonds as there is a chance of default.

- ***High-yield bonds*** – Commonly referred to as junk bonds, these corporate bonds are issued by companies with below-investment-grade credit ratings. The lower the quality of the bond the greater the likelihood of default.

If low interest rates have your income down, bonds or bond mutual funds could help to increase your cash flow.

ANOTHER IDEA TO UP YOUR INCOME

Collateralized Mortgage Obligations allow you to make a loan (just like all bonds) to an institution. The institution then lends the money out to homeowners to buy homes. A federal agency such as Fannie Mae, Freddie Mac or Ginnie Mae guarantees your security. You don't need to worry about whether the homeowner pays his/her mortgage or not. You will get your payment each month because the federal agency or federally chartered corporation guarantees your principal and your interest.

In fact, these securities have an "implied" AAA rating. Although they do not have formal ratings from rating agencies, many investment professionals consider these securities to have a quality similar to those with an AAA rating, because of the federal agency guarantee to payment of principal and interest. These securities have one significant difference as compared to treasury securities— the term of these securities is not fixed.

Hypothetical Example:

The average homeowner in the United States moves every seven years. So, you would expect that if you lent money to people to buy homes, you would get paid back in seven years, on average. However, when you lend your money in this fashion, it gets spread out and lent to many,

many homeowners. Your money gets automatically diversified. Some of those people are going to move in two years, some will move in five, but some are going to be in their homes, ten, fifteen and twenty years from now. Therefore, when you make this type of investment, you will be quoted an estimated life of your investment, which may be five years, seven years, eight years or more. That's the estimated time of when you can expect your money to be returned. Keep in mind that it is only an estimate and can change significantly. Therefore, you could incur costs of reinvesting and be at the mercy of market swings.

If you buy a Fannie Mae security or a Collateralized Mortgage Obligation that is guaranteed by Fannie Mae, and it has a five-year estimated life, you could see principal back in two years if some people who borrowed the mortgage money move very quickly. Other people will live in their homes for years and your money will continue to come in over the entire period. At all times your principal is guaranteed and you will receive the fixed rate of interest that was promised you. As long as you are investing part of your core capital in these types of securities, you could have a potentially attractive return. Not a bad place to permanently park some money.

PREFERRED SHARES

Corporations raise money by issuing preferred shares of stock, which are very similar to bonds. The primary difference is that preferred shares have no maturity date (similar to Collateralized Mortgage Obligations). Once you invest in preferred shares, you own them until:

1. You sell them
2. They are called by the corporation

Because they pay a higher rate of interest than bonds, many investors purchase preferred shares. Typically the rate is 1% more than bonds of the same company. The higher rate is due to higher risk in severe cases. If the company ever had financial problems, the bondholders would get paid first, before the preferred shareholders. Since the preferreds are second in line to be paid if the company liquidates, the preferred shareholders take more risk and are better paid. As a practical matter, if you buy high-quality preferred shares (these ranked by S&P just as bonds are ranked), such companies are not likely to go into liquidation.

Generally, preferreds are issued at $25 per share. You can invest in these shares when they are first issued or anytime by purchasing them on the stock exchange. Make sure that you check the call feature. I have seen many investors buy preferred shares that paid a high current dividend that did not realize they bought the shares at $30 per share and the call feature allowed the company to call the shares the following year at $25. These investors experienced a whopping $5 per share loss because they did not check the call feature.

Preferred shares pay dividends every quarter. For investors who want to have their income keep pace with current market conditions, there are adjustable rate preferreds. These shares do not have a fixed dividend, but rather have a dividend that is usually based on treasury bill/bond rates. As the interest rates move up or down in the economy, so will the investor's income. There is usually a minimum and maximum rate that is guaranteed. If you find a minimum rate that is attractive, you can invest and sit tight when interest rates rise and potentially collect more income.

REAL ESTATE – A POOR CASH FLOW INVESTMENT?

Rental property has always been a popular investment because of its appreciation potential and leverage. But in many parts of the country, it can be of a poor cash flow investment.

Hypothetical Example:

Assume you own a rental home with a $250,000 value, free of debt. You receive rent of $1,200 per month. After expenses (including those periodic expenses of replacing the roof, adding an air conditioner, painting), you net $800 per month. If you sold the property, you would receive $188,000 after taxes. Now let's put these numbers together. Your net $800 per month ($9,600 per year) on equity of $188,000 (the amount you would have if you sold the property). That's an annual cash return of 5.1%. Is that cash return worth getting calls to fix the plumbing, chasing late rent checks or having to evict tenants?

Does it really make sense to own real estate? Yes, because the real estate appreciates. However, if you want to increase your cash flow, real estate may not be the ideal investment. As investors age, many become more interested in spendable cash flow and less interested in appreciation. An income-oriented investor may not want to deal with the difficulties of owning rental properties if they know they can get a better rate somewhere else without the work.

(Note: I often see people incorrectly prepare the above analysis based on the amount they originally paid for the property. To correctly see what you are earning, you must use the current equity because that's the amount of money you could invest elsewhere.)

PUT AWAY MORE MONEY WITH LESS HASSLE

Many people retire, get bored, and start up their own business. If you are self-employed, even if it is just part-time, you might want to look at a new retirement plan that will let you sock away a lot of cash (and reduce your taxes now) to support your later years.

Effective January 1, 2002, the Individual-401(k) allowed sole proprietors to put aside more pretax dollars than in other plans, such as profit sharing plans, money purchase pension plans, SEP IRAs, and SIMPLE IRAs. In some cases this could be more than twice as much.

The I-401(k) is designed for owner-only businesses and those with part-time or seasonal employees who can be excluded under federal laws governing plan coverage requirements. It's unique in that it combines the simplicity of an IRA along with the high contributions limits normally associated with a traditional 401(k). Unlike a traditional 401(k), it does not require costly administration, testing, and reporting.

Business owners can contribute up to 25 percent of their pay into an I-401(k). The most you can put away though is $40,000. However, if you are 50 or older, you can set aside even more in catch-up contributions. And if your spouse works in the business, he or she can also participate in the plan and take advantage of the same limits as you. Like the standard 401(k), you can borrow from an I-401(k) plan. And, you can do it without the troublesome administrative stipulations associated with the older plan.

Another feature that will make managing your retirement assets easier is the ability to consolidate your existing SEP or profit-sharing-plan balances into an I-401(k). You can put your I-401k, IRAs, rollovers and other qualifying retirement funds into one account. No separate accounts are needed.

Keep in mind that if you hire an employee, your contributions, as well as the complexity of the plan, may change. Nevertheless, if that happened, you could discontinue the I-401(k) and start a traditional 401(k).

REVERSE MORTGAGES

Seniors who are in a cash flow bind because of increasing expenses or a drop in their investment income may want to look at tapping into one of their most valuable assets, their home. There are several ways to get equity out of your home:

1. You could sell your home, but you would have to find somewhere to live.

2. You could borrow from your home. This may be a viable alternative as interest rates are the lowest they have been in decades. However, as interest rates rise this alternative becomes less favorable.

3. You could do a reverse mortgage. A reverse mortgage is a loan that allows homeowners over the age of 62 to convert the equity in their home into cash and still live there. You can receive your payout as a lump sum, as a fixed monthly income (up to lifetime), as a line of credit (to use at your discretion), or as a combination of these. The

amount of the reverse mortgage will have to be paid back with interest when you die, sell the home, or permanently move out. You or your heirs do have the option to pay off the reverse mortgage at any time and keep the house. Additionally, the repayment amount can never exceed the value of the home. And, if the sales price exceeds the amount owed, the excess will go to you or your estate.

There is no income or medical requirement to qualify for a reverse mortgage and you can use the proceeds in any way you wish (i.e. to pay living expenses, medical bills, or travel expenses). The size of your reverse mortgage is dependant on several factors:

a) Your age
b) The value of your home
c) Current interest rates

Hypothetical Example:

Bill age 65 and Marge age 63 own a home valued at $250,000. Health problems required Bill to close his part-time consulting business and the loss of Bill's income forced them to cancel a cruise they had been planning for the last year. A reverse mortgage offered Bill and Marge the following options:[6]

A. Single lump sum or line of credit: $140,285
B. Lifetime monthly income: $784

(The money you receive will be tax-free and will not affect your Social Security or Medicare benefits)

Bill and Marge chose the line of credit. They took out enough to pay for their cruise and kept the balance available for another vacation, for an emergency, or to supplement their income in the future.

Chapter Three

Mutual Fund Investing

Mutual funds allow an investor to buy a portfolio of stocks and bonds without having knowledge of the stock and bond markets. Additionally, they allow the investor freedom from the day-to-day monitoring of his portfolio. They provide diversification and management by professionals. Some investors do far worse than they should because they don't entirely understand what's going on with their mutual fund.

Carefully consider investment objectives, risks, charges, and expenses before investing. And please read the mutual fund prospectus. Many investors are unaware that a mutual fund prospectus can be used for more than leveling a coffee table.

BEWARE OF LAST YEAR'S BEST FUNDS

Some mutual funds reported annualized returns of 40%, 50% or more for 2003. Many investors decided to reinvest some of their sluggish funds into these "winners." And then, as soon as they got in, these "winners" turned to losers and started declining in value. Many investors feel that they might be financially jinxed, that as soon as they get into an investment, it declines. This losing experience results from the way mutual funds advertise their results, investors' behavior, and the "tendency toward the mean."

First, let's look at the way mutual funds advertise. When do you think a mutual fund company decides to advertise a specific fund, just after a losing period or a winning period? Typically, they advertise a fund right after it has had a great return (and often just as it's about to cool off).[7] You can avoid such situations simply by ignoring mutual fund advertisements. Often, well performing funds do not repeat their performance in subsequent periods. As Russel Kinnel, director of fund analysis with Morningstar said, "Had you used the (1999) top-10 performers' table as your shopping list, the best you could have done from January 1, 2000 through March, 2003 was lose a little more than half your money."[8]

In fact, the least popular fund categories have done better than the best performing fund categories as reported in an annual Morningstar Study.[9] Every January since 1987, Morningstar Fund Investor finds the three least popular fund categories from the previous year determined by net cash flow; inflow vs. outflow.[10] Since 1987, the least popular funds have outperformed 90% of the most popular funds over the following three years.

Sometimes the investor can be the problem. Investors will often jump into a fund after it advertises a very good period. Once investors are on board, the fund performance weakens. This is generally a problem when a fund is new and small. When a fund starts out it is maneuverable and may show a good track record. Its small size enables it to invest in smaller, potentially rapidly-growing companies without owning an excessive amount of a small company's stock.[11] Once investors attracted by the good results pile in, the fund can lose its maneuverability. Its increased size forces the fund to seek out larger companies in which to invest its larger sums. These larger companies tend to grow much less rapidly than their smaller company counterparts. As pointed out by Russel Kinnel, this "hot streak" phenomenon is often followed by a steep decline in the fund's performance.

The other problem is a statistical phenomenon called "regression toward the mean."[12] As it applies to mutual funds, it means that mutual fund categories will all perform about the same over the long term. Some categories will do well for a period of time, beat the market and then do poorly over the next several years and underperform the market. All funds are cyclical in this way. For example, biotechnology funds will do well for a while and beat the market. Then they will have a period of terrible performance. You can observe the same cycle for most any fund category, such as Pacific Rim Funds (great in the early 90s, terrible in the late 90s), REITs (poor performance in the 80s, much better in the 90s) and precious metal funds (significant performance in the 70s and 80s, terrible performance in the 90s). Over the long term, these categories all converge toward the average market return.

Be careful about chasing the advertised funds, as today's winner can be tomorrow's "dog." Your best defense may be an "all-weather" strategy. This strategy eliminates the need to jump in and out of hot categories and guess which funds are the "best" right now. An all-weather strategy puts you in the funds that are right for you and are changed only when your situation changes, not when a particular fund category looks "hot."

DATA SHOWS INVESTORS SELECT FUNDS USING INCORRECT CRITERIA

A Morningstar study looked at 5 years of fund data and found that although past performance was a very unreliable predictor of future performance "the connection between past risk and future risk was very powerful. The riskiest funds stayed the riskiest and the safest stayed the safest."[13] In other words, the data suggests that selecting funds by risk level is a lot more reliable. And when measuring risk, past risk did predict future risk.

Many investors select funds based on past return even though the more reliable indictor of the future is risk. A wise investor will manage their risk because they understand that they have no control over their returns anyway. Professionals do not guess at returns or make forecasts; they plot the probabilities. They seek to get the biggest return for the least amount of risk. And it is risk you can control. You actually know this intuitively if you've ever been in a casino. You can sit at the $10 table or the $100 table. If you selected the $10 table, you were managing your risk.

MUTUAL FUND FEES

Some mutual funds are loaded with fees. That's not necessarily bad. If the fund is making you a return that you're happy with, then high fees are not a problem. As an informed investor, you should understand the truth about the fees of any fund you invest in. You should know what you're paying. There are generally three types of fund fees (one of which is not evident in their prospectuses):

Management Fees - These fees pay the smart people who actually buy and sell the securities in your fund and do the investment research. In addition, these fees pay the accountants and attorneys who audit the fund, prepare the prospectus and provide professional oversight. These fees also pay the members of the board of directors. Also included are printing and postage expenses. All funds have management fees, as no fund will manage your money for free. However, some funds have management fees a lot lower than others. A few funds have fees less than 1/10th of 1%. At the other extreme, there are a handful of funds that charge their shareholders 3% annually and more.[14] Sometimes it pays to shop around.

12b-1 Fees - These are fees that the fund takes from your account to "distribute" the fund (advertise for new fund shareholders and pay securities brokers to provide you service). It may seem a little unfair that your money is being used so that the fund can attract new investors and have your securities broker convince you to remain in the fund, but that is what a 12b-1 fee does.

Turnover Costs - The prospectus of every fund shows you the fund turnover, but does not tell you what turnover actually costs you. Turnover measures how often the fund is buying and selling. A fund with 100% turnover means that it completely turned over its portfolio during the year. Turnover is important because it's expensive. As of 12/31/03, of the 15,986 funds in the Morningstar database, 5,118 had turnover rates exceeding 100%.[15]

Many factors affect turnover costs, including commissions, bid/ask spreads, taxation, and the size of trades. According to a study conducted in 2002 by Personal Fund, the average turnover cost was 1.9% for domestic equity funds. When you add up the management fee, the 12b-1 fee and the turnover costs, it's not hard for a fund to have total costs exceeding 3%. So if you have $50,000 invested in a fund with costs of 3%, that costs you $1,500 every year. That may not be so bad until you take a look at the taxes....

TAXES

In a non-tax deferred account (tax deferred accounts being IRAs, 401(k)s, 403(b)s etc…), when you buy individual stocks, you pay no capital gains tax until you sell your shares. Not so with mutual funds. Every time the fund sells a stock for a profit, you must pay tax on your share of the profit, even if you have not received a distribution. The gain incurred by the fund may be a long-term capital gain (taxed at federal rates up to 15%) or the fund may have short-term capital gains (taxed up to 35% as ordinary income). Each year you receive a 1099 form to report on your tax return and you pay taxes on these gains in addition to dividends.

Another irritation is that these taxes are even higher in years when the market falls and fund investors create net redemptions in the fund. When more fund shareholders want to sell than buy (which usually happens when the market is falling and investors get scared), the fund will sell its holdings in order to create cash to pay the selling shareholders. These sales of stock by the fund often create capital gains and these will be reflected on your 1099. So in years when you watch your fund decline in value, you may also get the biggest tax bill.

TURNOVER

The turnover rate in a fund is not necessarily a bad thing, but as mentioned, it does increase your tax bill if the fund is selling stocks with lots of short-term gains. Turnover can hurt a fund's return.

According to a recent study by Stefan Sharkansky, the lower a fund's turnover, the higher its returns, in general. "We analyzed the ten-year cumulative performance records of open-ended mutual funds in existence from

December 1991 through December 2001. Our findings are consistent with previous studies. On average... lower turnover funds outperformed higher turnover funds by a substantial margin in every category of funds that we studied."[16]

The study also found that for the 10 years ending 12/31/01, each 100% turnover was expected to reduce the performance of a large-cap fund by 1.24% and 2.55% for small-cap funds.[17] The conclusion of the study: "Although our study admittedly covers a limited time period, it makes a strong case that for many domestic-stock categories less active managers are more successful. Investors are particularly unlikely to benefit from high-turnover strategies among large-cap value and blended funds and the rewards of turnover are also fairly small for most other categories." (Please note that this study only analyzed the effect that turnover has on performance. High turnover also increases the investor's tax impact.)

TURNOVER AND TAXES OF FUNDS

Many investors own mutual funds, but few of them realize how much they really earn after taxes. Here's a little insight from *Creating Equity* by John Bowen. In a study commissioned by Charles Schwab and conducted by John B. Shoven, professor of Economics at Stanford University, and Joel M. Dickson, a Stanford Ph.D. candidate, taxable distributions were found to have an impact on the rates of return of many well-known retail equity mutual funds.

The study measured the performance of 62 equity funds for the 30-year period from 1963 through the end of 1992. It found that the high-tax investor who reinvested only after-tax distributions would end up with accumulated wealth per dollar invested equal to less than half (45%) of the funds' published performances. An investor in the middle-tax bracket would see only 55% of the performance published by the funds.

Another study, by Robert H. Jeffrey and Robert D. Arnott, published in the *Journal of Portfolio Management*, concluded that extremely low portfolio turnover can be a factor in improving a fund's potential after-tax performance. Asset class funds typically have very low portfolio turnover, which translates into less frequent trading and, therefore, may result in lower capital gains. Low turnover may also benefit shareholders by holding down trading costs.

The above studies indicate that you can lose a significant amount of your mutual fund returns to taxes and that funds with high turnover tend to generate higher taxes for you. Remember, it's not what you make, it's what you keep.

DERIVATIVES AND STYLE DRIFT

Did you know your fund might borrow money to buy securities? Many investors are uncomfortable knowing that their fund borrows money (in an effort to buy more stocks and enjoy gains), because it could magnify their losses if the market falls.

Derivatives - Most investors simply don't know if their fund uses volatile derivatives in order to boost returns. Derivatives are financial instruments, whose up and down price movements are based on the movements of an underlying security, such as a stock or bond. However, the derivative's volatility is much greater. If the stock moves 10% in value, the derivative could move 50%. These issues are mentioned in your fund's prospectus, but you may not know that your fund can be volatile until your fund's semi-annual report. The use of leverage by mutual funds can significantly increase a fund's volatility. Low-risk investors might want to steer clear of funds that trade derivatives.

Style Drift - You might invest in a value fund which focuses on large "blue chip" companies selling at modest price earnings ratios. What happens if the fund manager gets tempted by the fast increase in Internet stocks and starts allocating the fund's money into these investments? That may not be what you thought you were getting into. If each of your funds begin to drift into the others, you may not be as diversified as you thought you were. You can avoid this problem of style drift by using funds that can never vary from their stated style in the prospectus.

PUTTING TOGETHER A MUTUAL FUND PORTFOLIO

I don't recommend assembling a fund portfolio by selecting a bunch of funds that seem to have done well lately. Unfortunately, that's exactly what many investors have done. Based on the last six months of *Money Magazine* or whatever publication they prefer, investors often buy the funds highlighted in the editorial stories. The problem is, if those funds have all been rising together, they could likely all fall together if they are in the same sector. The goal should be selecting funds that are complementary to one another, so your overall return will be a smooth, rather than a concentrated boom or bust pattern resembling a roller coaster ride. (Note that there is no allocation or system to assemble a portfolio that will assure a profit.)

I have seen many investors that had several of the same stocks included in several of the funds they own. In such a situation, the investor understandably thinks they are diversifying (because they own several funds), when in fact, they are concentrating. I recommend that mutual fund investors analyze their portfolio of funds to determine the extent to which their funds are redundant rather than providing the diversification that they desire.

LOAD VS. NO-LOAD FUNDS

Investors can debate indefinitely whether paying a load (and getting the accompanying advice of a financial advisor) or do-it-yourself with no-loads is better. That conversation is rooted in the realm of people's opinions. I find the facts much more interesting.

Investors in no-load funds tend to be more fickle than those who buy through an advisor, according to a Morningstar Study (The Virtues of Commitment, 11/7/97 Morningstar Principia Commentary). For the three years studied, the net cash flows (an indicator of buying and selling) of no-load funds were 40% more volatile than load funds. You might think, "Those no-load buyers are smarter and sold to trade up to better performing fund." The data suggests that may not be the case.

In a previously mentioned study it was determined that the funds that were the *least popular with investors* (those funds experiencing the greatest cash outflows) typically went on to be the best performers for the next 3 years. It seems somewhat unlikely that these least popular funds were the funds that the no-load investors switched to. Remember, the more volatile the net cash flows of a fund the more difficult it is for the fund manager to generate a satisfactory return. The fund manager will need to trade more increasing turnover expenses and taxes, forcing them to sell into a down cycle when fund shareowners are cashing out.

Rather than selecting funds based on load vs. no-load, there are many more important criteria that can have a significant impact on your results.

ACTIVE VS PASSIVE FUNDS

John Bogle, founder and retired chairman of Vanguard Funds, criticized the mutual fund industry claiming:

- Mutual Fund managers are too short term oriented as they now hold a stock only 406 days as compared to 7 years in the 1950s

- Mutual fund expenses are rising

- Even though the return on mutual funds has been 17-18 percent annually during the past 15 years, after taxes and costs, the returns are only 11-12% annually, thereby cutting the investor's accumulation in half

As many know, Bogle popularized the index fund (passive fund) concept claiming that index funds have far lower fees than actively managed funds and as a result, a lower tax bite and better overall performance. So does the data prove him right? Quite often it does.

The chart on the top of the next page shows the comparison of actively managed equity funds as compared to the performance of the S&P 500 index for the 17 years ended 12/31/99. In only 3 of those years did the actively managed funds beat the index. However, in 1999, that started to turn around, as actively managed funds started to pull up.

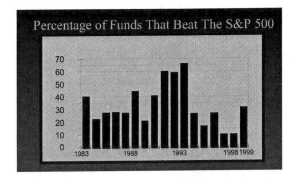

Strong performance by technology stocks has also helped fund managers beat the indexes. Many index funds track the S&P 500, which doesn't have many tech names, while actively managed funds can overweight technology stocks which at times have been "hot."

Another problem has been the S&P 500 has been slow to change. It took the index until December 1999 to add Yahoo (YHOO) and America On Line (AOL).

So which way should you go, passive or actively managed funds? It may make sense to use index funds when you want part of our portfolio exposed to a large group, such as large cap value funds. When it comes to focusing on specific arenas such as micro cap, technology, biotech, country specific funds or other sectors, active management could provide the extra value you seek.

WHEN TO SELL A MUTUAL FUND

"When is it time to sell?" Throughout my career this has been one of the most common questions I am asked by investors. It's a reasonable question, but many investors may not like the answer. Here are 5 questions to ask of each fund you own:

1 Has the fund under-performed its peer group during the last 3 years. You can determine this from a number of on-line sources or major fund reporting services such as Morningstar or Weisenberger.

2 Has the manager changed? You can find this out by calling the fund directly. The fund manager is an extremely important variable in fund performance.

3 Have the expenses or turnover changed? The easiest place to look is Morningstar.

4 Have the assets grown too quickly? The semi-annual report you receive shows the changes in assets managed. Typically, but not always, a fund can have difficulty keeping up its past record when it grows too quickly.

5 Has the fund strategy changed? You can determine this by comparing the investments the fund holds over time, or read the prospectus to determine any changes in philosophy.

It may take some time but you should assess your portfolio in this way at least once a year to determine if in fact there are funds that you should be selling.

TAXATION ON THE SALE OF A FUND

Investors who receive statements directly from their mutual fund company should save their December statement. These statements show the total reinvested dividends for the year and all other transactions. Other mutual fund investors receive statements from the brokerage firm. Save every monthly statement as these statements may not accumulate the total of your reinvested dividends each year. Without these statements you will not have the information you need to calculate the taxes when you sell. For many, the lack of statements often leads to overpaying your taxes.

Hypothetical Example:

You invested $50,000 into a fund that has grown to $150,000. On its face you gained $100,000. Most would assume that you would pay tax on the entire $100,000 gain. However, if you had reinvested a total of $40,000 of dividends throughout the years, then your actual investment is the original $50,000 plus the $40,000 of dividends. Your total amount invested would have been $90,000. Instead of paying tax on $100,000 gain, you should have paid tax on a $60,000 gain ($150,000 value today less your total investment of $90,000).

If you do not have the statements, either the fund company or your brokerage firm may be able to provide them. If you inherited the shares, the calculations can get somewhat complicated. Your original investment of inherited shares is the value on the date of the benefactor's death.

Hypothetical Example:

You owned 10,000 shares of ABC mutual fund: you bought 6,000 shares and inherited the remaining 4,000 shares. When you sell shares, you can select which specific shares are sold. This is only a paper exercise where you report the purchase date to the IRS the specific shares you sold. The flexibility of being able to select specific shares can save a lot of money. By picking the shares with the highest cost and the lowest gain you pay the lowest tax.

MUTUAL FUNDS VS. VARIABLE ANNUITIES

There has been a lot written about the tradeoff between costs and tax savings of variable annuities. With mutual funds, you have the problem of the taxes you pay each year even in years that no distributions are made. Additionally, if you switch from one fund to another, even in the same mutual fund family, you create a taxable event. Some variable annuities may complicate this issue even further by offering some additional features.

People invest in variable annuities for many reasons of which tax-deferral of earnings is certainly one. Variable annuities can offer investors' an income stream they can never outlive as well as the ability to avoid probate. Sometimes investors overlook an important option that may help them plan for a predictable income.

The Guaranteed Minimum Payment (GMP) option assures that you will receive no less than a specific amount of income each month, no matter what the markets do. And if the investments go up, your monthly income goes up too. Insurance companies determine the GMP option in various ways. In each circumstance the GMP option is based on the financial strength of the issuing company. One example of how this benefit works is to offer the investor the greater of:

- The value of your purchase compounded at 6% a year, or

- The highest account balance reached on any contract anniversary date

Another version of the GMP option promises that future payouts will never be less than 75% of their first payment. If your first check is for $1,000, future distributions will be no less than $750 regardless of what happens to the markets, even if your account value went down to zero. However, if the value of your annuity increases so do your payments. Additionally, you are not required to annuitize your account (give up control) to receive this benefit and you can withdraw your money as a lump sum at any time.

Variable annuities enable you to select from variable accounts that can closely resemble your mutual fund portfolio. In addition, you can switch between these accounts without having to pay taxes. The criticism of variable annuities is that the total annual expenses are generally higher than most mutual funds.

The investor can be left with a dilemma. Do the higher expenses of a variable annuity (2.09% annually vs. 1.4% in the average mutual fund according to the August 1999 Kiplinger's Retirement Report) justify the savings of tax deferral? And does the tax deferral justify the fact that some of the funds withdrawn from variable annuities will be taxed at ordinary rates while some of the taxes generated by mutual funds are taxed as long-term capital gains?

Before you decide, consider the following questions:

- Will you use the variable annuity primarily to save for retirement or a similar long-term goal?

- Are you investing in the variable annuity through a retirement plan or IRA (which would mean that you would not receive an additional tax-deferral benefit)?

- Do you understand the features of the variable annuity?

- Do you understand all of the fees and expenses of the variable annuity?

- Do you intend to remain in the variable annuity long enough to avoid paying any surrender charges?

- If a variable annuity offers a bonus credit, will the bonus outweigh any higher fees and charges annuities charge?

- Are the features of the variable annuity, such as long-term care insurance, something that you could purchase less expensively on your own?

- Have you consulted with a tax advisor and considered all the tax consequences of purchasing an annuity, including the effect of annuity payments on your tax status in retirement?

- If you are exchanging one annuity for another, do the benefits of the exchange outweigh the costs?

INDIVIDUALLY MANAGED ACCOUNTS VS. MUTUAL FUNDS

Financial firms of all types – from banks to securities firms to insurance companies – are frequently recommending individually managed accounts as opposed to mutual funds. Before reviewing the differences, it's important to understand that an individually managed account is not a portfolio designed just for you. The professional manager handling the investment of your account may have 5000 people with the same portfolio that you do.

Unlike mutual funds however, you do have your own account and your money is never commingled with the accounts of others. Now that we know the basic difference, here are the issues to consider:

1 Capital Gains tax can be more favorable in an individually managed account as you often have the flexibility to delay a sale of a stock until the following year. With mutual funds, you do not have such flexibility. This is especially important to note as short-term gains generated by many funds are taxed at ordinary rates up to 38% federal.

2 You minimize the influence of other investors when you have an individually managed account. In a declining market, fearful investors might want to sell. Mutual fund investors desiring to sell their shares for cash force the fund manager to sell shares in the fund to raise cash. In other words, the manager may be forced to sell in a down market. With an individually managed account, no other investors influence sales in your account.

3 Reporting is often more comprehensive, clearer and more frequent in an individually managed account.

4 Fees of individual accounts and mutual funds vary greatly so a general comparison is not possible. It is however possible to compare the fees of a given mutual fund against a given individually managed account. When calculating the costs of a mutual fund, remember to include the management expenses, any loads, 12b-1 fees and the costs associated with portfolio turnover.

5 You get more personalized service with questions answered by a knowledgeable professional when you have an individually managed account. Typically, when you

call a mutual fund company, you speak to a customer service person that is far removed from the management of your fund.

Individually managed accounts typically require a $100,000 minimum investment. Investors looking to invest smaller amounts may not have this as an alternative.

FREE ONLINE RESOURCES

There is no substitute for carefully reading the prospectus of a mutual fund or variable annuity before making a purchase. Regulatory agencies such as the NASD and Securities and Exchange Commission (SEC) offer a variety of free online resources to assist the investing public. Here are a few:

• **SEC Mutual Fund Cost Calculator** – www.sec.gov/investor/tools/mfcc/mfcc-int.htm

• **SEC Mutual Funds** – www.sec.gov/answers/mutfund.htm

• **SEC Variable Annuities: What You Should Know** – www.sec.gov/investor/pubs/varannty.htm

• **NASD Investment Choices** – www.nasd.com/ Investor/Choices/investment_choices.asp#invmf

• **NASD Variable Annuities: Beyond the Hard Sell** – www.nasd.com/Investor/Alerts/ alert_variable_annuities.htm

• **NASD Understanding Mutual Fund Classes** – www.nasd.com/Investor/alerts/alert_mfclasses.htm

Chapter Four

Qualified Retirement Plans

Retirement plans (IRAs, qualified plans, 457 plans, and tax-sheltered annuities) are very complicated and few people realize it. For many, a retirement plan is simply about putting money away to get a tax advantage, using the money during retirement and leaving anything that's left to the kids. Banks and brokerage firms are always advertising "invest your IRA with us and we'll help you to achieve your retirement goals." Why is it that you rarely see an ad that says, "We will show you the best way to take money out of your IRA for the least amount of tax?" One reason you don't see ads like this may be that banks and brokerage firms don't make money by saving you money on taxes.

Many investors pay a great deal of attention to how they invest their IRA, but ignore the "end game," when the IRS splits the IRA with you through taxation. When you know the details, you can earn more on your retirement plan, pay less tax on withdrawals, avoid common mistakes in naming your beneficiaries and get more overall benefit from your retirement plans.

REQUIRED MINIMUM DISTRIBUTIONS

Every so often bills are neglected or paperwork is overlooked. Statements can get lost in the mail or you may have forgotten to send in the forms. Generally the company will just tack on a late fee or overlook the delay. The IRS is not so generous, especially when it comes to your required minimum distributions (RMD).

IRA owners must start taking RMDs no later than April 1 of the year after they turn 70½. Each December 31 thereafter, they must do the same. Failure to follow these rules can be very expensive.

IRA custodians are obliged to tell the treasury department how much your IRA distribution is supposed to be for that year. If you miss taking a distribution or take one that is less than required, you must take the missed distribution and pay a 50% penalty on that amount. Because distributions do not get special consideration as dividends or capital gains, they are considered ordinary income, assessed at your highest federal and state tax rate. The penalty and income tax could possibly total more than 85%.

Never Take More Than Your RMD

Most investors have two pots of money, the money that has already been taxed ("regular money") and the money that has not yet been taxed ("retirement money" such as IRA, 401k, 403b, etc.). When you spend a dollar of regular money, the cost to you is exactly $1. When you spend $1 of retirement money, the cost to you is about $1.33 because you need to pay approximately 33% of income tax on the amount you withdraw.[19]

If you want to reduce your taxes, consider taking only the required distribution amount from your "retirement money" even if it means you must spend down your "regular money" principal for living expenses. Many investors believe that they should never spend their principal. This can be a mistake if you want to save money on income taxes. Look at the money in your pocket, it's all green. Interest and principal are just ideas. When you look in your bank account you cannot tell which is which. It can be better to spend your "regular money" principal that has already been taxed and allow your untaxed "retirement money" to grow as much as possible. You might be better off from an income tax standpoint. Your lifetime tax bill can be less or you will at least defer taxes for many years.

As you can see from the chart, starting with $200,000, you can have $150,000 more by spending your regular money and holding on to your "retirement money." You will eventually pay tax on your "retirement money" when you use it later in life, or your heirs will pay the tax when you are deceased. The good news is you get to hold on to more of your money while you're alive.

Spend Regular Money First

	Today	In 20 Years
Spend Regular Money First		
Regular Money	$100,000	$40,916
IRA Money	$100,000	$320,713
TOTAL	$200,000	$361,629
Spend IRA Money First		
IRA Money	$100,000	$0
Regular Money	$100,000	$211,247
TOTAL	$200,000	$211,247

Assumptions: All money earns 6%, combined federal and state income tax is 33%, illustration over 20 years, distributions of $6,000 annually, tax on IRA withdrawals also deducted from IRA account, mandatory IRA distributions not assumed.

From Which Account Should You Draw First?

Typically, you would want to take money from your taxable accounts first to preserve the tax deferral of your retirement funds. There may, however, be circumstances in which investors should consider alternatives.

When you withdraw funds from a taxable account, your income tax liability is limited to amounts exceeding your initial investment. In most circumstances all of the money you distribute from your "retirement funds" is taxed as normal income. However, if you let your "retirement money" continue to grow, you may pass on a potentially larger tax burden to your beneficiaries. This is an especially important consideration for those with a majority of their assets in "retirement plans."

If you use your "retirement funds" first, you will have to pay the income tax. This would however, enable you to keep a greater amount of the taxable accounts intact to transfer income-tax free to your heirs. It can be a tough choice to make and everyone's situation is different. Here are two alternatives you may want to consider:

Convert to a Roth IRA

You could roll your "retirement funds" to a Roth. This is not a tax free transfer. You will have to pay income tax on the amount transferred. Once the funds are transferred, withdrawals and bequests are income tax free. There are two important variables may help you determine if converting to a Roth IRA is right for you:

1) **Do you have cash available to pay the taxes with non-IRA funds?** You will pay the income tax on

your already accumulated IRA balance, and the conversion will only make sense if you can transfer the entire amount of your existing IRA to a Roth and use non-IRA funds to pay the taxes.

2) **Will you be able to let the money continue to grow without withdrawal for at least five years?** If you will need to take more than nominal amounts (e.g. interest), then converting to a Roth IRA is probably not the right thing for you. The benefit of the Roth IRA is the tax-free accumulation of the assets. If you need to use the assets within 5 years, you will not allow for the necessary accumulation to make the conversion worthwhile.

WEALTH REPLACEMENT TRUST

Many retirees have benefited from increasing home values and investment values in the 1980s and 1990s. As a result, some estates have grown to a size that they now may be subject to estate tax. "Retirement plans" may be subject to two levels of taxation: income tax (rates up to 35% in 2005) and estate tax (rates up to 48% in 2005). Compare your income tax liability of taking money from the taxable account vs. the "retirement funds." And, consider the tax bill your beneficiaries will face. Assuming you qualify, you may want to buy a life insurance policy to offset the income tax and potential estate tax burden for them.

Hypothetical Example:

A single IRA owner age 70 has a seventeen-year life expectancy.[20] He has a $1 million IRA growing at 10% annually. He takes only the minimum distributions each year. By life expectancy, his

IRA balance will be $2,315,270.[21] The IRA will be subject to income tax at rates up to 35% and estate tax up to 48%.

Plan Balance	$2,315,720
Income Tax (33% assumed for this example)	$ 764,187[22]
Estate Tax (2005 IRS rates)	$ 376,545[23]
Net to Heirs	$1,174,988

50% of the IRA value is lost to taxes. By taking only the required minimum distributions today, our investor has created a huge estate tax problem for tomorrow.

What if instead of taking only the minimum distribution, our IRA owner distributes an additional $19,373 annually from his IRA. He would pay an additional tax of $6,393 based on a combined tax bracket of 28% federal and 5% state. He could invest the remaining after-tax amount of $12,980 in a life insurance policy (owned outside of his estate).[24] At his death, he would leave his heirs a death benefit of $500,000, income and estate tax free.[25] Of course, the IRA balance will be smaller due to the distributions to pay for the life insurance.

Plan Balance	$1,810,637
Income Tax (33% assumed for this example)	$597,510
Estate Tax (2005 IRS rates)	$139,786
Life Insurance death benefit	$500,000
Net to Heirs	$1,573,341[26]

If your current plans involve leaving an IRA to your family, you may want to consider this technique for leaving your heirs potentially much better off.

Stretch IRAs

Recently there has been much discussion regarding "stretch" IRAs, the concept of allowing your beneficiaries to spread out the tax on the portion of your retirement dollars that you leave to them. Continuing from our previous hypothetical table, if your $100,000 retirement fund grew to $320,000 and you died before spending any of it, your heirs would receive the $320,000. They can then keep the money in the IRA without spending it and continue to defer taxation until age 70½.[27] This sounds great but typically it does not happen. There are two things that can prevent this from ever happening: your heirs and your IRA custodian.

Heirs - At your death, your heirs could remove the entire balance in one lump sum and buy a yacht. By taking a lump sum they will pay all of the tax at once and lose years of tax deferral. One way to control this is by not leaving your IRA assets outright to heirs. Instead, you may want to leave the assets in an IRA trust. In a trust, you can control exactly how the funds are distributed to your heirs.

IRA Custodian - Your IRA custodian may also change your plans by inadvertently acting against your wishes. Your custodian may have rules such as "all distributions to heirs must be paid out in 10 years." If your funds are in a 401k, the plan may also force a fast payout, making the stretch concept impossible to implement for non-spouse beneficiaries. Your IRA custodian may even go so far as to disinherit your grandchildren:

Hypothetical Example:

You have two sons, Jack and Tom. You name them as primary beneficiaries for your IRA when you open the account by completing an "IRA Beneficiary Designation Form." As shown below, Jack and Tom each have a son. Jack's son is Bob. Tom's son is Dan. You decide to put your grandson's names on the line of the beneficiary designation form that says "secondary or contingent beneficiaries."

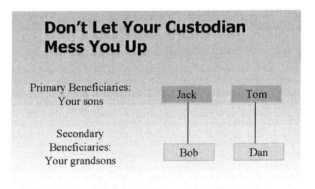

Don't Let Your Custodian Mess You Up

Primary Beneficiaries:
Your sons — Jack — Tom

Secondary Beneficiaries:
Your grandsons — Bob — Dan

If Jack were to die before you did, you need to know what would happen to Jack's half of your IRA when you pass away. Most people would think it goes to his son, Bob. If the beneficiary designation form did not specify how the beneficiaries and secondary beneficiaries were related it could go to Tom, leaving Bob out of the picture. It is not uncommon that beneficiary designation forms would not provide a place to specify how the primary beneficiaries and secondary beneficiaries were related or to explain your intentions and your desires with respect to those beneficiaries. The beneficiary designation form that you filled out with the bank or the securities firm may not be sufficiently detailed to carry out your wishes.

You may want to give your IRA custodian complete instructions on your own form. These forms are known as "Retirement Asset Wills" because they provide a complete set of instructions regarding your retirement assets. A knowledgeable attorney can help you in preparing this.

Ask Your IRA Custodian These Questions:

- Will the custodian or plan administrator accept as valid a detailed, customized beneficiary designation form or will they require that the designation of a beneficiary or beneficiaries be done on their own forms? A custodian or plan administrator's own form is often too limiting. Be prepared to sign a document relieving the plan administrator or IRA custodian of liability for accepting your customized form.

- In the event of death, will the custodian permit your beneficiary or beneficiaries to receive payments over the period permitted by tax law and IRS rules and regulations, or will they mandate a shorter payout period?

- In the event of death, will the custodian permit your beneficiary or beneficiaries the amount of time granted by the tax law or IRS rules and regulations to choose among any available options, or will the custodian require a choice be made in a lesser time?

- In the event of death, will the custodian permit your beneficiary or beneficiaries to do a trustee-to-trustee transfer of the IRA account to a different custodian?

- In the event of death, will the custodian permit the beneficiary of any portion of the account, to name a subsequent beneficiary, for the sole purpose of avoiding probate in the estate of the beneficiary, in the event the beneficiary should die prior to the exhaustion of the account balance?

- If at the time of death, your beneficiary or beneficiaries are permitted (by their election or other-wise) to take distributions over a certain number of years, will the custodian permit distributions over that period even if a beneficiary should subsequently die? For example, if, at death, the beneficiary is permitted a payout period that computes to 40 years, the tax law locks in that 40 year pay-out period, even if the beneficiary should die sooner.

Please be aware, some retirement plan custodians may refuse to take your custom instructions. If you encounter this problem with your custodian, you may want to find one that will accept your instructions. In most cases retirement assets are freely transferable from custodian to custodian. The same flexibility applies to a beneficiary who inherits an IRA and finds the custodian has a rule to payout the IRA quickly rather than allow the stretch concept. Again the beneficiary can transfer to a more flexible custodian.

MISTAKES IN SELECTING BENEFICIARIES

When most people select beneficiaries for their IRAs, they select their spouse or their children. As simple as this may seem, it can create problems. Consider these two scenarios:

Scenario 1 - When you leave an IRA account to your spouse, it inflates his or her assets. If he or she later dies with an estate exceeding $1.5 million (the estate exemptions limits in 2004 and 2005), they pay estate tax. By leaving them your IRA, you have created unnecessary estate taxes by making their estate larger.

Scenario 2 - You chose to leave the IRA to your son, he may withdraw the funds immediately and decide to buy a mansion jointly with his spouse. Let's say that the following week, your daughter-in-law files for divorce and gets to keep the mansion in the settlement. You would have given your ex-daughter-in-law a mansion with your IRA money.

In an effort to avoid the above two scenarios many people decide to leave their IRA to their estate. Natalie Choate, one of the nation's foremost authorities on IRAs, advises that you never leave your retirement plan to your estate.[28] The IRS' stance is that an IRA owner's estate cannot be classified as a designated beneficiary.[29] Rather than enjoy the potential "stretch" over their lifetimes, the IRS requires your beneficiaries distribute the account over an extremely short period of time. Additionally, the IRA will now be a probate asset subject to claims of creditors.

What might you do to avoid these problems? You may want to leave your IRA to a trust. Within the boundaries of your wishes and IRS-required minimum distributions, the trustee of your trust is empowered to decide who among your beneficiaries will get the IRA and how much they get. The trustee is empowered to decide how quickly the money is distributed over and above the annual minimum amount of required IRS distributions.

You have the ability to leave very detailed instructions. If you desire the money to be used for education you may want to stipulate that up to $15,000 a year can be distributed for education expenses or $25,000 to start a business. You can go on and on with such instructions. If you would like a say in how your retirement plan gets used and distributed, you should consider leaving it to a trust rather than directly to a person.[30]

IF YOU HAVE CHARITABLE DESIRES...

If you desire to leave even $1 to charity, do it with money from your "retirement plans." You can specify one or more charities to receive portions of your "retirement plan" and your other heirs will thank you. When you leave your heirs a dollar of IRA funds, they will pay approximately 33 cents to tax, leaving 67 cents left to spend.[31] If your estate is over $1.5 million, your heirs will also pay estate tax on this money. This may leave your heirs with only 35 cents of each dollar.[32] When you leave your heirs a dollar that is "non-retirement" money, they can spend it without paying income tax.

For every $1 of "retirement money" that you leave to charity, the charity receives $1. There is no income or estate tax to consider as charities do not pay tax. By appropriately allocating your retirement funds and post-tax funds correctly to charitable and non-charitable beneficiaries, taxes can be saved.

WHAT INVESTMENTS SHOULD BE IN YOUR IRA?

Investment Options

Inside IRA	Outside IRA
■ Growth Mutual Funds	■ Index/Low Turnover Mutual Funds
■ Short-Hold Stocks	■ Long-Hold Stocks
■ Taxable Bonds	■ Tax-Free Bonds

What should be in your IRA and which investments outside your IRA? If you own growth oriented mutual funds, own them inside your IRA. The average growth mutual fund has a turnover rate exceeding 100% a year.[33] A mutual fund must hold a stock for more than 12 months to get the most favorable capital gains treatment. High-turnover funds will often hold stocks for less than 12 months. Stocks which are held for less than 12 months are subject to "short-term" gains. The maximum tax on short-term gains is 35% as opposed to the "long-term" capital gains tax of 15%. High turnover and high tax funds are often better suited for your IRA where you will be shielded from tax.

Mutual funds with low turnover, such as index funds, tend to hold stocks for more than 12 months and may benefit you more holding them outside of your IRA. Keep municipal bonds outside of your IRA. Municipal bonds generate a lower return than taxable bonds. Many investors are willing to accept this lower return for the promise of tax free income. By holding municipal bonds inside of your IRA you would be making this low return taxable.

By appropriately positioning your money inside and outside of your IRAs, you may be able to lower your tax burden and increase the return on your investments.

USING LOWER STOCK VALUES TO YOUR BENEFIT

Most people have heard of the Roth IRA. And, as the tax on the conversion is due immediately, it is understandable why few seniors have chosen to exercise this option. However, if the investments held in your IRA have lost value, it may be the time to pay this alternative a little more attention.

When your IRA balance is down, you can convert to a Roth IRA and pay tax on a reduced value. For the first 5 years after converting to a Roth IRA you may withdraw principal tax free, but withdrawals of earnings would be subject to tax (If under age 59 ½, all withdrawals would be subject to penalty). After 5 years distributions are tax free (principal only if under age 59 ½).

Not everyone can take advantage of the Roth conversion. Your adjusted gross income must be under $100,000. Should your AGI exceed $100,000, you might be able to make adjustments to drop your income for that year (i.e. those people with a business or income in their control may be able to drop their income for one year).

This conversion is better for people who prefer to have growth oriented investments in their IRA and plan to use a good portion of their balance during their lifetime. In addition to tax-free distributions from a Roth IRA there are some other benefits. Unlike traditional IRAs, Roth IRAs have no required minimum distributions at age 70 ½. Also, because tax on Social Security income is calculated on your total income (total income – Roth IRA distributions) you may pay less tax on your social security income. If you are married, it is not uncommon for household income to remain the same when one spouse dies. Because single people are taxed more heavily than married people on the same income, the surviving spouse might be pushed up into a higher tax bracket. Tax-free distributions from a Roth IRA may enable them to remain at their lower tax bracket.

ROTH CONVERSION MAY STILL BE A VIABLE ALTERNATIVE

Even with depressed account values most investors will never convert from a traditional IRA to a Roth. Tax-free distributions would be nice, but paying tax immediately upon conversion makes this option out of the question for most investors. But, what if you could reduce this tax or even push it off until after you die, would you at least consider it?

You can reduce the tax by purchasing a fixed annuity in your IRA and then converting to a Roth IRA. The IRS rule states that you are to pay tax on the fair market value of assets in your IRA when you convert. An annuity is taxed at its "surrender value," rather than at its higher "account value" when distributed from or converted to an IRA. By owning the right investment, you can reduce the taxable amount of your IRA.

There still remains the problem of the immediate tax payment, albeit smaller by using the annuity. There is a way to avoid taking the money from your pocket. For those who are determined to maximize the cash flow from the conversion, you may want to use a residential equity line to pay the tax. Many financial institutions offer equity lines, interest-only, at prime rate. Most people can deduct this interest and pay it with a tax-free withdrawal from their Roth IRA. As long as your investments outpace the prime rate, you are ahead. You will get a tax deduction and have your IRA grow tax-free. You can pay off the equity line when your house is sold. If you live in your current house for the rest of your life, the equity line is paid from the house proceeds, and your heirs inherit a tax-free Roth IRA after your estate is settled.

HUGE TAX SAVINGS FOR THOSE ABOUT TO RETIRE

Many retirees have employer stock in their 401(k) and profit sharing plans. In these cases, there is an opportunity for converting ordinary income (taxed at rates up to 35%

federal plus state) into capital gains income (taxed at only 15% federal plus state).

Rather than rolling over their employer stock into an IRA, you may want to take actual distribution of the shares. You will pay tax at ordinary income rates on the basis of that stock. The basis is the value of the shares when they were originally put into the plan. When you eventually sell the shares, you will be taxed at capital gains rates (15%) on the unrealized appreciation of the stock only. If you were to rollover the shares into an IRA, you would pay ordinary income tax on the entire value of the shares.

Hypothetical Example:

Joe Smith has a 401(k) plan at ABC Manufacturing Company. He invests his contributions into company stock during his tenure for a total investment of $100,000. By the time Joe is ready to retire, the shares are worth $600,000. Joe has two options:

Option 1 – Joe decides to roll over his shares of ABC Company into an IRA. When he reaches age 70½ he must begin taking distributions from his IRA, paying taxes on those withdrawals at ordinary income rates up to 35% federal plus state. He will pay these full rates on all of his shares. Assuming no further appreciation above the $600,000, Joe would pay tax of $210,000 on the shares (35% federal rate plus state).

Option 2 – Instead of rolling the shares into an IRA, Joe decides to take them as a distribution and pays tax of $35,000 immediately on the basis (35% of $100,000). Later, when he sells the stock (at his discretion because he is not subject to the age 70½ rule) he pays a capital gains tax of $75,000 (15% federal tax of $500,000). Rather than $231,600, Joe's total federal tax bill is only $110,000. That's a savings of $120,000 in federal tax, enough to pay for plenty of great vacations for Joe and his wife.

If you have employer stock in your company retirement plan this may be a strategy for paying a lot less in taxes.

ROLLING OVER YOUR IRA—OTHER CONSIDERATIONS

Many people roll their company 401(k) or other company retirement plan into an IRA to obtain total control over the assets (e.g. you can choose from any stock, bond, mutual fund, or annuity). While this is generally a good idea, there are some other important considerations:

A balance in an ERISA plan (401(k), profit sharing, pension, etc.) is protected by federal law from bankruptcy and alienation. If you get sued or declare bankruptcy, your ERISA plan balance is protected. This protection disappears however, once you roll over your ERISA plan into an IRA. It is then up to your state government or judicial system to determine how your IRA gets treated in the case of bankruptcy or creditor pursuit.

IRAs cannot own life insurance. There are some very powerful techniques for saving taxes by placing life insurance in a non-IRA retirement plan and then distributing that policy at a reduced tax basis. You can however, convert your IRA into a qualified plan, to enjoy these additional tax saving and estate planning options.

IRS Rule Might Prevent Depleting Your IRA

Many early retirees have taken advantage of the "substantially equal periodic payments" provision in the tax code to avoid the 10% early withdrawal penalty from their IRA. This special exception requires that you calculate the amount you intend to distribute and stick with that plan for five years or until you are 59½, whichever comes last.

For years this concept worked out very well. Recently, with a declining stock market, many retirees have seen their IRA balances shrink while their required distributions remain the same. They now must cope with the possibility of draining their accounts many years sooner than they had originally anticipated.

On October 3, 2002, the IRS issued an announcement that has helped this group of retirees.[34] The IRS will now allow you a one time change, without penalty, to a method of calculating their payment amount that is based on the value of their account as it fluctuates from year to year. You are now able to recalculate the required payout each year by dividing the account balance for that year by the number provided by life expectancy tables for that year.[35] Whether or not this new ruling can work for you will depend on the amount your IRA has dropped in value, your age, and how far you are from the end of your required payments.

How to Help Your Grandchildren Learn about Investing

Many people would like to provide financial support to their grandchildren. Isn't spoiling young grandchildren with an overabundance of gifts one of the benefits of being a grandparent? Once they reach their teens, what approach should you take to temper their material demands and teach them how to make solid financial decisions?

It is not uncommon to find that your grandchildren do not know how to balance a checkbook or understand the concept of interest charged on credit card debt. Do your best not to get too frustrated. Less than one half of high school graduates have had a course in economics, which leaves many of them without the knowledge needed to become informed consumers and investors.[36] The good news is that teens are becoming more aware of the importance of preparing for the future.

According to the Investment Company Institute, the number of minors who hold Roth IRAs has practically doubled.[37]   The flexibility of Roth IRAs makes them especially beneficial for working teens; contributions can be withdrawn for college expenses, and up to $10,000 can be used for first-time homebuyers.

If your grandchildren aren't interested in saving for their retirement (40 to 50 years away) you can make the contributions on their behalf as long as they do not exceed the child's actual earned income or the $4000 maximum allowed contribution (Grows in increments to $5,000 in 2008). Share with your grandchildren how their money will be invested and review their investment statements. Over time they will see their accounts grow. Sooner or later they will start to appreciate the benefits of investing.

If your grandchild has no earned income, you may want to consider hiring them to work in the family business or to do real work around your home (i.e. painting or mowing the lawn). Be sure to keep records of when the work was done, just in case the IRS asks.

It's a great idea to get your grandchildren involved in their financial futures and teach them about long-term savings and how the markets work.

Chapter Five

Long-Term Care

The health care system in the U.S. is designed to handle acute illnesses. Acute illnesses are those illnesses that doctors can fix by checking you into the hospital, fixing you and then releasing you from their care. Illnesses however, are not always compatible with this system. Often times, illnesses will be long-term and debilitating in nature. Typically, your insurance will not cover these long-term costs resulting from the illness (i.e. Limitations of Parkinson Disease, Extra Care Needed to Deal with Chronic Arthritis, Incapacity of Multiple Sclerosis, Disability Caused by Stroke, Care Needed Due to Alzheimer's).

Nearly 10% of people over the age of 65 in the U.S. have purchased long-term care insurance to cover these costs.[38] At $4,000 per month for long term care, a person can accumulate a fairly significant long term health care bill rather quickly.[39] While most seniors would never consider being uninsured for routine health care, many are content to close their eyes to the risk that their health insurance won't cover the entire list of possible afflictions. I urge you not to ignore this risk, as I have seen far too many heart-breaking financial hardships. It is important to realize that a major reason to address the issue of long term care is to protect your family.

Why You Don't Want Government Support in Your Old Age

It is not uncommon for someone in a discussion about long-term care to say "I'll just go on Medicaid." The government developed the Medicaid system as a last resort. For many people across the country, Medicaid may be their only option. Others may choose to explore other alternatives and many including the California Advocates for Nursing Home Reform would argue for good reason:

"While spending down is easy to do and to document, it may be difficult to find a nursing home placement if you have no resources and must find a bed in a Medicaid-certified facility. The longer you pay as a private patient, the more options you have when looking for a nursing home. In most areas, Medicaid pays less per day than the amount a facility will charge a private pay resident...In some cases, while Medicaid discrimination is illegal, facilities have been unwilling to accept residents who are eligible for Medicaid upon admission."[40]

Unfortunately these stories of discrimination against Medicaid residents are not at all uncommon. Michael McDermott, a Maryland health care consultant, describes the issue:

"When the mayor of a city walks into a restaurant, there's no policy that dictates he or she will get the best table, the thickest steak and superior service at the expense of other patrons. But that's what often happens. The same thing is occurring in nursing homes. Any nursing home operator will pick a private-pay patient over a Medicaid patient. This attitude filters down to the staff and it affects Medicaid patients' quality of life on a day-to-day basis."

If you want quality care for yourself or your family members, do not depend on government support for it; instead, be prepared to pay for it. At least be prepared to pay for three years of care from your own pocket to help obtain placement in a quality location. Additionally, while Medicaid will not provide long-term care in the home, with your own funds or private insurance, you can be covered to provide care in your own home.

DO YOU NEED LONG-TERM CARE INSURANCE?

Almost half of the people over the age of 65 will spend some time requiring long-term care.[41] With such a high risk, one could easily conclude that everyone would need insurance. Especially once you consider that the cost of long-term care can run well over $4,000 a month.[42] The fact of the matter is, many people may not need to buy insurance and I'll explain why. I generally divide people into three groups:

Group #1: Total assets under $300,000

Group #2: Total assets $1 million and over

Group #3: Total assets over $300,000, but less than $1 million

Group #1: This group has a lower net worth and could have a difficult time making the annual premium payments for insurance. These people may be better off organizing their assets so that they can qualify for Medicaid. Medicaid will support you once you have spent all but around $2,000 of your liquid assets (this amount can vary by state).[43] There are however, ways to shelter assets from Medicaid so that you can get support without spending down all of your assets.

Group #2: This group probably has sufficient income and assets so that they can comfortably handle a monthly expense of $4,000 or more.[44] Many of these people do, however, obtain insurance. It enables them to protect their estate from being depleted by a long-term care need and gives them independence by providing a separate source of funds to be used should they need long-term care.

Group #3: This group may need the insurance. They generally have too much net worth to qualify for Medicaid, yet they do not have enough to handle the expense of long-term care without depleting their assets entirely. Draining $4,000 or more per month from anyone in this group will erode their estate or, in the case of a married couple, could create an income hardship for the healthy spouse. If you are in this group, you may want to consider the insurance. Long-term care policies are often used by people with significant assets that want to preserve their estate for family members, assure independence and not burden family members with nursing home bills.[45]

How Much Long-Term Care Insurance Do You Need?

When it comes to any type of insurance, you should consider how much of the risk you can afford to pay out of your own pocket and how much you want to pass off to the insurance company. The more you're willing to pay out-of-pocket, the lower the insurance premiums. The problem with long-term care planning is that you have no way of knowing how incapacitated you're going to be or how long you'll need the care. Every case is different. I would strongly encourage you to do an analysis of your financial and personal situation. Include the cost of long-term care in your state, your life expectancy, and what tradeoffs you may be willing to make.

Hypothetical Example:

- You and your spouse have a combined income of $50,000 ($20,000 from Social Security and $30,000 from a pension).

- This income of $50,000 covers all of your expenses.

- You have savings and investments totaling $300,000 averaging a 7% rate of return over the past five years.

- The average annual cost of a nursing home stay is $50,000.

If either you or your spouse needed long-term care, the spouse still at home may have a difficult time surviving. You could withdraw 7% a year ($21,000) from your investments in an effort to preserve principal. There would still be a $34,000 shortfall. If you were to take out the full $50,000 a year, assuming the portfolio averaged a 7% rate of return, your portfolio would be gone in less than seven years.

An alternative to make up the $34,000 shortage would be to purchase a long-term care policy with a $95.00 a day benefit ($34,675 per year). You may want to provide a slightly higher daily benefit as there is no guarantee your portfolio will continue to earn 7% a year. It all comes down to how much risk you are willing to assume.

WHEN SHOULD YOU GET INSURANCE?

If you determine that you need the insurance, I recommend you obtain it as early as possible. The longer you wait, the more expensive it gets.[46] Many people attempt to save money to prepare for a long-term care need rather than investing in insurance. If they never need nursing care, they have successfully avoided paying the insurance premiums every year. However, should you need long-term care it is somewhat unlikely that you could save enough to equal the benefit provided by an insurance policy.

Hypothetical Example:

A 50 year old man started saving $680 per year for his future long-term care needs. With his savings returning 4% annually, he would accumulate $38,000 over the next 30 years. In the year 2030 the cost of the average stay in a nursing home may be well over $495,000.[47] That same amount invested in a long-term care insurance policy would provide a benefit of $828,000 for long-term care.[48] Certainly, it is better to start a policy earlier because the premiums are typically lower. Much more importantly however, is that you need to qualify for coverage. As you age and the probability of adverse medical conditions becomes greater, you run the risk that you will not qualify for insurance.[49] Even notations in your medical records, whether they are accurate or not, can make you uninsurable.

Two Important Reasons to Get Long-Term Care Insurance

To whom will you turn if you are stricken with a long term debilitating illness? Often people are uncomfortable asking their spouse to bear this burden, concerned that they would turn their spouse's life upside down, from an easy retirement to a dreary existence.[50]

If you are single, your children may feel obligated to help you. Assisting a sick parent can be a full time job. Feelings of resentment can sometimes build as your children try to fit helping you into their already overworked schedules, although, they would never say so.[51]

In addition, you could very easily spend down your assets entirely leaving your heirs with nothing. There has been much confusion over the years as to why you should address the problem of long-term illness. It is to insure your family's quality of life and to preserve your independence. Many people would have great difficulty asking their children to brush their teeth or asking them to determine how to spend down your assets for your care.

Insurance is simply an alternative for those who do not have sufficient assets on their own to create a separate pool of money to be used for care inside or outside of the home. Further, it enables you to maintain your independence.

The Facts Reveal Misconceptions

The Health Insurance Industry Association conducted a decade-long study titled *"Who Buys Long Term Care Insurance in 2000."* The facts from the report diverge from many commonly held myths:

- *Myth:* Long term care insurance is for old folks.
- *Fact:* One third of people who obtain long term care insurance are under the age of 65.

- *Myth:* Long term care insurance is bought by people who are not financially sophisticated.
- *Fact:* Buyers of long term care insurance policies are typically wealthier than non-buyers.

- *Myth:* The government will pay.
- *Fact:* Non-buyers are twice as likely to have this misconception.

- *Myth:* Long term care insurance is expensive.
- *Fact:* The average premium paid in 2000 was $1677. This was only an 11% increase over a five-year period.

- *Myth:* I would buy if the premium was deductible.
- *Fact:* Non-buyers were three times more likely to be unaware that under many circumstances, premiums are tax deductible.

- *Myth:* I'll just have my kids take care of me.
- *Fact:* Long-term care continues to be the largest, single out-of-pocket expense faced by the elderly and their families. In addition, many children do not have the time and would rather not take care of an ill parent.

What's It Cost?

The cost for long-term care insurance can vary widely among both the companies and types of coverage. Different companies charge different amounts for different benefits. One company may charge more than another for inflation protection and be less expensive for home care. There is no single company that is the lowest cost for all benefits. The first step is to decide on the benefits you want. Then you can then determine which company is best for you. There are five important items to consider when choosing coverage:

1. **Inflation Protection** - This protection will increase your insurance benefit over time to keep pace with the rising cost of long-term care. The younger you are, the more important this benefit is. The cost of long-term care is increasing rapidly. I would strongly encourage anyone who is under age 75 to consider this benefit as it will hopefully be many years until they will need long-term care.

2. **Benefit Period** - This option determines how many years the insurance company will pay you benefits once you need them. You choose the term of your coverage. Typically, I recommend that people apply for benefit periods of 4 years or more. Fourteen percent of the people who need nursing care need it for 5 years or more.[52] By selecting a benefit period of at least 4 years, you have enough coverage to cover 86% of long-term care incidents.

3. **Daily Benefit** - This is the amount the insurance company will pay you per day to cover your care. I recommend a minimum daily benefit of $100 per day. That would give you $3,000 per month.[53] If your actual cost is higher than $3,000 a month, you will probably be able to cover the cost among the insurance, your Social Security and other income sources.

4. **Coverage for In Home and Outside the Home Care** – This feature allows you to determine where you would like to be covered: inside your home, outside your home, or both. While many people like the idea of receiving benefits while remaining in their own home, the more important insurance is for outside the home (e.g., nursing home or assisted living facility). There are two reasons for this:

a) In home care is usually more moderate (i.e. shopping, cooking, cleaning or bill paying) and typically costs less for such non-medical help. Often, friends, neighbors and family can lend a hand, making it much easier financially to cover in-home care. When at home care is no longer sufficient and outside the home care is required, the costs can increase exponentially. That is when you really need the insurance.[54]

b) The design of your home may not enable you to stay at home if you are ill. Stairs, long distances to the car and narrow doorways can all present problems for people using a walker or who are in a wheel chair. Often, it just makes more sense to obtain care outside the home in facilities designed more appropriately for these needs.

5. **Elimination Period** – This is the number of days you will pay for care before the insurance starts to pay. Most policies allow you to select between periods ranging from zero days to 180 days. Similar to your car insurance deductible, the more you are willing to pay for a loss out of your own pocket, the lower your insurance premium. A 90 day elimination period is most common as people are willing to pay

for some of the care to keep their annual insurance premium reduced.

Consider coverage for in-home and out-of-home care as your budget allows.

FIVE WAYS TO REDUCE THE COST OF LONG-TERM CARE INSURANCE

Often people who need long-term care insurance will choose to go without it. Generally, cost is the biggest issue and for good reason: it's not cheap.

While I believe in having complete coverage, it may be better to have at least a basic policy than having nothing at all. None of us know when a health catastrophe can strike. A stroke, cancer, Parkinson's and Alzheimer's are debilitating illnesses which can give little to no advanced warning. Protect yourself and your family financially. Here are five ways to get covered at a lower cost:

1. **Reduce the coverage period.** Reducing the term of the policy from 4 years to 3 years can provide a significant savings. And, a 3-year policy covers 72% of the cases of long-term care.[55]

2. **Reduce the daily benefit.** The average cost of nursing care is $155/day.[56] If you cover just $100 or $90 per day with insurance the premium is noticeably reduced. Some people find that they can make up the difference with other income sources, such as Social Security or interest income.[57]

3. **If you are age 75 or over,** you may want to consider omitting inflation protection. Hopefully, you will

never need long-term care. However, if you do, you are more likely to need it within 10 years (age 85). The cost of long-term care may not increase sufficiently to warrant the purchase of inflation protection.

4. **Consider partial home care coverage.** Many people desire the "in-home care" benefit but are not willing or able to afford it. A few companies offer partial coverage for at home care (i.e. $100 per day outside home benefit and a $50 per day in-home benefit). By reducing the benefit for home care, you can lower your insurance premium and have a reduced coverage for at-home care.

5. **Eliminate home care insurance.** Many people have a spouse or friends or relatives who can assist them with long-term care inside their home. Hired home aides are another alternative and are relatively inexpensive ($18.12 per hour).[58] At-home care may be more easily covered within the means of your own income.

RETURN OF PREMIUM

I have yet to meet anyone who would enjoy needing long-term care and many people argue that the money invested in insurance premiums is wasted if they never use it. Some insurance companies have addressed this issue by creating a policy that pays back at least what you put in, whether or not you need long-term care.

This optional feature offered by only a few long-term

care insurance companies may be the answer. The return of premium option promises to refund 100% of your premiums if you die before using your entire long-term care benefit. Your refunded premiums will go directly to your beneficiary.

ONE CHECK FOR LONG-TERM CARE INSURANCE

Instead of paying premiums annually, the policyholder may want to make one premium payment and be done. These policies are sometimes referred to as "combo" policies because they offer 2 benefits, long-term care insurance and life insurance. Unique to this type of policy is your ability to get back 100% of the premium paid at any time.

Hypothetical Example[59]:

65 year old female

Single Premium Payment $50,000

Long-Term Care Insurance Benefit $281,664

Life Insurance Benefit $ 93,888

The policy provides the following features:

- She can surrender the policy at any time and receive back at least the total of her original premium (less loans, withdrawals, fees, and expenses). While she has the policy, she earns interest and has both life and long-term care insurance.

- If the policyholder dies, her heirs will receive the $93,888 life insurance benefit (less loans, withdrawals, fees, and expenses).

- Should the policyholder enter a nursing home or need home health care, she would receive up to $281,664 in long-term care benefits (payments reduce the death benefit and payments are reduced by prior loans, withdrawals, fees, and expenses).

Depending upon which situation applies, the policyholder or her heirs will collect the original premium in one of three ways:

1. Long-term care insurance benefit

2. Death Benefit

3. Withdrawals

This plan of insurance may be an alternative for someone who would like long-term care protection but does not think they will ever need it.

You Might Not Need Any Cash

If you have an older life insurance policy with a substantial cash value you may be able to do a tax-free exchange into a life/long-term care policy without spending any money out of your own pocket.[60] Be aware, your old policy may be subject to surrender charges. Another option would be a partial, tax-free surrender for the amount of money that you had put into your old life insurance policy. You could use that money to buy a standard long-term care plan.

The Immediate Annuity Solution to Long-Term Care

Often I meet investors with small amounts of money in fixed annuities. Annuities have a feature (annuitization) that is similar to a pension, in that it allows you to receive monthly income payments that are guaranteed for life.[61] Assume you have an annuity valued at $20,000. Such an annuity might generate a lifetime payout of $1,300 annually. By committing this small asset, you would be able to fund your long-term care premiums for life. If you are uninsurable for long-term care insurance, immediate annuities may be able to help you in another way.

The state government, through Medicaid, will pay for your long-term care needs only when you have less than $2,000 in liquid assets. In other words, they will help, but only when you have nothing left. There are however, ways to appear broke without actually being broke.

When immediate annuities are purchased within Medicaid guidelines, they are considered non-countable assets. You can keep the asset and still qualify for Medicaid payments. The government would require that you return a portion of each payment to pay for your long-term care, and you get to keep the rest.

Which Insurance Company is Best?

Many insurance companies have excellent policies, but there is no "best" company. Some companies will offer better rates than others for the coverage you select. Other companies may provide better rates to people who are in their 70s than to people in their 50s.

As we discussed earlier, the first step in purchasing long-term care insurance is to decide on the benefits that are most important to you. It becomes much easier to determine which insurance company best suits your needs once you know what you're looking for.

Just because you want long-term care insurance doesn't mean you can get it. The insurance company will need to review your medical history to determine if you can get it and what it will actually cost. If you get insurance, you can always cancel it. However, if your health fails, you may be uninsurable.

Unfortunately, many investors feel best about a financial decision when everyone else is doing the same thing. "There is safety in numbers." Often there can also be ignorance and foolishness in numbers. Whether others are acting to protect themselves does not alter the facts. Of every 100 people who have attained the age of 65:

- 43 will have a need for long-term care assistance, either in the home or a facility outside of the home.[62]

- 36 will need long-term care for more than 4 months.[63]

- 5 will need long-term care for more than 5 years.[64]

READ THE FINE PRINT

Before purchasing long term care insurance, it's important that you make a thorough comparison. The fine print in policies can make a big difference in many of the benefits you select. It is not uncommon for policies to define your maximum payment as the lesser of your daily benefit or your actual expense.

Hypothetical Example:

You have a benefit that will provide you a $120 maximum daily benefit. If on Monday, you were to have someone go to the supermarket for you and they spent $20, your policy would cover that. The following day, you get 8 hours of care for a total cost of $200. Your combined bills for Monday and Tuesday were $220. Even with a two day benefit totaling $240 ($20 more than your actual expenses) you would be responsible for paying $80 out of your own pocket. Each day is measured by itself, it is not cumulative.

There are policies that measure the benefit per week. Rather than a $120 per day benefit, the benefit would be a cumulative $840 per week. By using a weekly measure, you can spend various amounts each day. If your total qualifying expenses for the week are less than $840, you will be reimbursed for all expenses that qualify under the policy.

Another consideration is how the policy counts the waiting period or "elimination period (the number of days you must pay for care before the policy starts paying)." Some policies start counting the first day you pay for care, but count only those days you actually pay for care. If you pay for care just once per week, it would take you 90 weeks (assuming a 90 day elimination period) until the policy would begin paying. Other policies will start counting from the first day you pay for care, it doesn't matter if you are actually paying for care each day.

If you have been considering purchasing long-term care insurance, before jumping into a policy, make sure you thoroughly understand how it works.

Do This In Advance

Frequently, people will wait until someone needs nursing care to explore the assisted living facilities and nursing homes in their area. You may want to see what options are available while your family is healthy and there is no pressure on them to make a quick decision. The alternative is to make a decision under pressure and with limited time. Often poor decisions are made in this way.

Sometimes a family member will become ill and regress rapidly. A patient suffering from such illness can age 3 years in a ten day hospital stay. It quickly becomes evident that there is very little chance they will be able to remain at home. The doctor recommends the closest nursing facility. Pressured to make a decision, you take the doctor's recommendation. Two weeks later you find that the nursing facility staff is incompetent and potentially harmful to your family member.

By doing a little investigation now, you can potentially avoid a scenario which gets repeated over and over. Ask friends or neighbors if they know anyone in a care facility and ask them about the treatment and service. You may want to visit those with the best reports.   With a few hours of time, you can narrow down the field of best care facilities to one or two.

A NOT SO BIG TAX BREAK

The federal government decided it could not afford to finance long-term care coverage for seniors so it announced a tax break. By giving a tax break, it would assist seniors in buying their own long-term care insurance. Many are concerned that this tax break might be more rhetoric than substance. Upon closer inspection you may in fact be worse off by pursuing this tax break.

The tax law allows anyone who buys a "qualified" long-term care policy to deduct the premiums. In addition, the government promises that when you receive benefits from the policy, the benefits will be non-taxable. However, there are limits to the deduction. The long-term care premium must be added to your regular medical expenses, and you can deduct only the amount that exceeds 7.5% of your income.

Hypothetical Example:

You have an annual income of $40,000. Your annual medical expenses are limited to $500 in non-covered prescriptions and $2000 in qualified long-term care insurance premiums. The total of your premium and medical expenses is $2,500 or 6.25% of your annualized income. You cannot deduct your premium because your total medical expenses are less than 7.5% or your income. In this instance, the deduction is simply rhetoric.

We must still address the taxability of your benefits. Up until 1997, benefits from any long-term care policy were tax free. The government has remained silent as to whether the benefits from qualified and non-qualified policies are tax free anyway. Since the government never changed the old law, many accountants advise their clients to consider the benefits from any long-term care policy tax-free.

LONG-TERM CARE PANIC

Recently, many people have received notices from their insurance company informing them that its long-term care policies have been sold to another insurer. Will you be dropped? Will the rates go up? Should you start shopping for a new policy? There has been consolidation in the long-term care insurance industry, but there is probably no need for alarm. Some people may in fact benefit if a more reputable and more stable company purchased your long-term care insurance policy.

Unlike the life and health insurance industries with decades of statistics to estimate future claims, long-term care insurance is a business with a short track record. This has made it difficult for companies to determine how much to charge for premiums. If the premiums are too high, consumers will not buy the policies. If they are too low, the insurer loses money.

Due to an inability to come up with a rate structure to adequately meet both these needs, some companies have gotten out of the long-term care insurance business altogether. Your new company will not drop you, nor will they change the terms of your policy. They can raise the premiums for an entire class of policies, but they cannot pick and choose which individual policies will get rate hikes.

Whether or not they will increase your premium depends largely on how the original rates were calculated. There are insurers that charge more for policies but do not raise premiums for a set number of years. If your policy was significantly less expensive than other comparable products, you will have a greater chance of getting hit with a price increase.

Moving from one company to another is generally not a good idea. When you apply to a new company, they will base your rate on your current age and since you'd be older than when you purchased your original policy, you would pay a lot more to start up a new one.

Rate increases with your new company may come in one large hike, or more frequent, smaller ones. Historically rate hikes have been infrequent and have ranged from 5% to 20% for the top eight insurance companies.[65]

Annual costs average $66,153 nationally for nursing home care and are higher if specialized needs must be met.[66] To protect your assets and maintain your financial security from the possibility of these devastating costs, long-term care insurance may be one of the best investments you can make.

Chapter Six

Asset Protection

No matter how well you invest or make financial decisions, your financial acumen and discipline is of no use if you let your nest egg get destroyed by catastrophe. When prepared you may be better equipped to avoid some of the financial heartaches in life that result from these unexpected occurrences: deaths, catastrophic illnesses, earthquakes, floods, etc.

WHO NEEDS LIFE INSURANCE?

Different situations will require different types of life insurance as well as varying amounts. In many cases life insurance is not required at all. Someone who is retired with only one dependent will generally require less insurance than the breadwinner of a family of six. The amount of life insurance you need is based largely on your family status, age, and economic situation. In addition, it is important to consider the costs and evaluate the benefits, as well as to understand ramifications of not having it. A "needs-based analysis" is one of the best ways to get an idea of how much life insurance is appropriate for you. It will give you a clear picture of your survivor's situation in the event of your death by a thorough review of the following:

- **Life insurance proceeds** – It is important to identify the amount your survivor(s) will receive from current life insurance policies. Be sure to include policies that you may have through your employer or those policies which are a part of your retirement package.

- **Assets** – Consider which assets your survivor could convert to cash quickly to provide for income or to pay final expenses. This may include retirement plans, real estate, mutual funds, and bank accounts. If the estate is subject to estate taxes (Federal & State), the IRS requires payment within 9 months and in cash. For many, this may not be a sufficient amount of time to sell a piece of real estate or a business.

- **Special bequests** – There may be gifts that you would like to make to charities or to pay for a grandchild's education or to assist a loved one in starting a business.

- **Outstanding debts and final expenses** – Upon your passing, mortgages, automobile loans, credit cards, medical bills, and estate taxes can be tremendous burdens to your family.

- **Annual expenses** – Determine how much income would be required by your survivor (including taxes) each year. Review your current expenses and deduct only those that will be eliminated after your death. Do not just cut your expenses in half; the cable bill is the same regardless of the number of people watching the television.

- **Annual income** – What sources of income will your survivor be eligible to receive. This may include Social Security, pensions, annuities, rental income, and salary. Determine which sources of income are protected from inflation. Social Security and many pensions offer cost-of-living adjustments to account for inflation.

- **Survivor's age** – Industry mortality tables can provide you with guidelines as to how long your survivor might live.

- **Rate of return on assets** – Figure out what type of investor your survivor would be (conservative, moderate, aggressive). A 2% or 3 % difference on investment returns can have a huge impact on your survivor's income over a ten or twenty year period.

Knowing the answers to these questions will help you to understand how much life insurance you need.

TERM VS. PERMANENT INSURANCE

One of the most common questions asked of insurance agents is whether it is better to buy term rather than permanent (whole life, universal life, and variable universal life) insurance. Many people prefer term insurance simply because it is less expensive than permanent insurance. Your decision about insurance should focus on the total cost, not just the cost in the beginning.

Term insurance is designed for temporary use. A parent with minor children might purchase term insurance while their children are still young and living at home. Similarly, business partners will often buy term insurance on each other. If they intend to sell the business within 15 years, they may want to protect themselves during that period in the event of the other's death. In these instances, term insurance is absolutely an appropriate choice. In some cases, there is a need for permanent insurance.

Hypothetical Example #1:

A husband has a large pension that ceases when he dies. The loss of the pension would create a financial hardship for the wife. The alternative is to select a pension option that would provide a benefit to his wife in the case he dies before she does. However, by providing this benefit, they would be forced to live on thousands of dollars less per year. Many pension plans provide this feature internally. However, the cost of purchasing an insurance policy on his own is often much less expensive and provides a greater benefit to his wife. Term insurance could work, but his wife would be in a real bind if he died the day after the policy ran out. The husband would be better served to purchase permanent insurance because we are uncertain as to how long he will live. The husband may live 3 years or he could live 35 years.

Hypothetical Example #2:

As homes and investments increase in value, there is growing concern regarding the amount and subsequent payment of estate taxes (federal & state). The cost can and will be substantial for many (up to 48%). Again, the term is unknown, and permanent insurance should be used. Permanent insurance needs can only be prudently funded with permanent insurance.

Term insurance is much less expensive in the early years, while permanent insurance has a stable premium.

The cost of term insurance rises with age. Additionally, your chance of acquiring coverage decreases with age. At some point in time, as we age, we all will be uninsurable. Use term insurance to address temporary needs (known periods of time) and permanent insurance for needs with indefinite periods (unknown).

INEXPENSIVE PROTECTION FOR YOUR SPOUSE

Many retired couples are dependent upon two social security checks or two pension checks to pay their annual living expenses. When one spouse passes away, the surviving spouse may find that their income has fallen substantially. The inexpensive way to protect against this situation is to own term life insurance.

Hypothetical Example:

A 70-year-old male buys a $100,000 policy for $115 a month. If he dies at age 80 and predecease his wife, she would receive $100,000 income tax free. This $100,000, invested at a 6% rate of return would generate $6,000 annually, enough to offset the loss of his social security check. Using 6% of principal and interest she would generate $17,000 for 7 more years.

There is certainly a chance the husband could outlive the insurance, however, we are much more concerned with the prospect of his passing in the nearer future.

Why Insurance Policies Lapse

Just because you own permanent insurance, doesn't mean it will necessarily be there when you need it. Over the last fifteen years, many seniors have purchased insurance policies as an estate-planning device. By using the life insurance proceeds to pay estate taxes, the remaining estate can pass to their beneficiaries intact and avoid the erosion caused by taxes. Some of these life insurance polices have "blown up." A little understanding can help you avoid this circumstance.

Hypothetical Example:

A gentleman approaches an insurance agent about purchasing a $1 million policy to offset his estate tax liability. The agent told him the premium would be $25,000 annually. Unwilling to pay this amount, the gentleman declined the offer. The agent responded, "what if we could knock the premium down to $12,000. How can the agent make the same policy available for less than half the price?

The lower price is not the same policy. When you receive a quote on permanent life insurance, you will always be given a "guaranteed" column of numbers and a "projected column" of numbers. The projected numbers are based on today's interest rate environment. When you purchase an interest-sensitive life insurance policy, the assumption is that the policy's cash value account will generate enough interest to pay the future premiums (the internal cost of insurance goes up as you age). This is not always the case.

If interest rates hold steady or rise, there will be

sufficient interest earnings on the cash value account to keep the policy in force. However, if interest rates fall, you can only count on the guaranteed column of figures. The guaranteed column is your "worst case" scenario. The guaranteed column may show that the policy "blows up" at age 80. If you live beyond age 80, the insurance would not be there (assuming that interest rates fall to the guaranteed level and stay there). If you want to guarantee that your insurance policy will be around as long as you will, then you must pay the higher premiums. You can get a policy that looks the same for half price, but you risk it running out before you do.

If you have purchased a policy in the last fifteen years, while interest rates have been declining, get a "policy ledger" from the company and review it. The ledger reveals if and when your policy will run out. Life insurance can be extremely beneficial under the right circumstances. Understand the worst case scenario and know that the "best" (price) quote may not be your safest quote.

WHAT SHOULD YOU DO WITH OLD LIFE INSURANCE POLICIES?

Sometimes, people own life insurance policies they may no longer need. The insurance was originally purchased when their children were young and their mortgage was higher. In retirement, with children grown and the mortgage paid down substantially, they may no longer have a need for the policy. If this sounds similar to your situation, you may have several good options:

1. You could do a tax-free exchange into a "combo policy," which would provide life and long-term care insurance protection. There would be no additional

cost to you unless you wanted to increase the death benefit amount.

2. You may want to surrender the policy for its cash value. Be careful, any cash you receive in excess of premiums paid is taxable to you.

3. Selling the policy is always an option. In many cases, you can sell a policy for more than the current surrender value. This works by having a life insurance agent bid for your policy in what is called a "senior settlement." The person who purchases your policy is hoping to make a profit when they collect the proceeds upon your passing. The worse your health profile, the higher someone may be willing to pay for your policy. Time will tell if they made a good investment or not (it is of no matter to you as you were paid upfront).

4. You may be able to leverage the cash value in your current policy into another policy with a higher death benefit. Often, older policies provided lower amounts of insurance compared to the cash value. In many cases, you can exchange this old policy (at no cost or tax to you) for a new policy that has a much larger death benefit.

SENIOR SETTLEMENTS

Among the more recent investments being touted by insurance agents as having a "high return with no risk" is the "senior settlement." With retirees on the lookout for high earnings and safety, "senior settlements" may be the answer. It depends largely on which side of the equation they fall: selling your life insurance policy to someone or purchasing the life insurance policy of someone else. The following will focus on the pros and cons of investing in the insurance policy of someone else.

In these arrangements, the investor provides a lump sum of money to buy a life insurance policy on the life of someone who is looking for money now. When the insured person dies, the investor, who is now the beneficiary of the policy, receives the entire death benefit.

Hypothetical Example:

Mrs. Jones has a number of illnesses and high medical bills, which she cannot afford. Additionally, she has a life insurance policy with a $100,000 death benefit. Mrs. Jones decides to sell her insurance policy to an investor for $60,000. She is pleased that she will be able to live more comfortably for the time she has remaining. If Mrs. Jones were to die the following year the investor would collect the $100,000 death benefit for a 66% annual rate of return. If on the other hand, Mrs. Jones lives another 5 years, the investor must wait 5 years to receive their $100,000. Their average annual rate of return would have dropped from 66% for one year to a 10.7% annualized average over 5 years. Although companies specializing in "senior settlements" retain experts to estimate the remaining life of the insured, they are still estimates. A patient with AIDS who is diagnosed to have two years to live, could still live for ten more years.

Investing in the insurance policies of others is an appropriate practice for investors who do not need the liquidity. The ultimate safety of the money may be fine, but be aware that you do not know when the payoff date will occur.

Chapter Seven

Taxes

Although most people would like their accountant to give them helpful tax savings strategies, many accountants do not. Some accountants will, in fact, prepare your tax return without providing the necessary advice to assist you in the future. A thorough analysis of your financial situation may yield some extremely favorable tax-savings. Examples of the kinds of savings you can uncover are as follows:

- Mutual funds generating more short-term gains (taxed as normal income) than long-term gains (taxed at lower rates)

- Opportunities to sell securities and avoid capital gains

- Higher than necessary IRA distributions

- Unnecessary payment of taxes on social security income

- Opportunities to increase current income

- Improper investment of bypass trust assets, where one spouse has died

- Opportunities to remove money from IRAs or pension plans at substantially reduced taxes

If you are tired of paying more tax than necessary and would like to keep more of what you make, it is time to do something about it. Remember, it's not how much you make that's important but rather how much you keep.

CAPTURE THIS TAX BENEFIT EACH YEAR

Every year, thousands of investors in stocks and mutual funds miss the benefit of tax loss selling. As an investor, you have the ability to have the government share in your investment losses by reducing your taxes.

Hypothetical Example:

A stock you bought at $20 is now worth $15. If you have been planning to hold it for the long term, now might be the best time to sell. By selling this year, you can report a $5.00 per share loss on your tax return. You can take a deduction or use it to offset other stock gains and reduce your tax bill or receive a refund. If you still want the shares, you can buy them back in 31 days and keep them as long as you like.

The government will not share in paper losses. You must actually make a sale to capture the tax benefit. Make it a ritual; sell your losers each December and have the IRS share the loss with you.

THREE WAYS TO BEAT TAXES ON SOCIAL SECURITY INCOME

As retirees well know, the federal government takes back part of your social security through taxes. Depending on your level of income, up to 85% of your social security benefit can be included as normal income on your tax return. There are some ways around this.

The general approach is to defer income. Deferred income does not appear on your tax return, it is not part of your taxable income and can increase the amount of social security benefit you keep. **Please Be Aware**, Tax free income will not help. Tax free income (i.e. municipal bond income) is included when the government calculates the tax on your social security benefits. Here are some sources of tax deferred income that can help to minimize the taxable portion of your social security benefit:

Annuities – These are vehicles for accumulating wealth on a tax deferred basis. Unlike CDs or mutual funds where you are taxed each year on the growth, annuities allow you to defer the tax. Annuities are issued in terms as short as one year and can help to reduce or eliminate the tax on social security income.

E Bonds – These are tax deferred savings bonds that offer extremely low interest rates. These rates are so low in fact that they may offset any tax savings.

Zero coupon bonds – There are a few issues of corporate zero coupon bonds that have tax deferred status.

Hypothetical Example:

	Scenario #1 Interest from CDs	Scenario #2 Interest from Tax-Free Bonds	Scenario #3 Fixed Annuity Interest (Non-Distributed)
Interest	$10,000	$10,000	($10,000)
Pensions	$25,000	$25,000	$25,000
Social Security Income	$20,000	$20,000	$20,000
Total Income	$55,000	$55,000	$45,000
Social Security Subject to Tax	$6,850	$6,850	$1,500
Adjusted Gross Income	$41,850	$31,850	$26,500
Total Federal Tax	$2,956	$1,456	$903

Source: TurboTax 2003[67]

The person who pays the least tax on their Social Security Income and the least tax overall is the annuity investor. The interest on reinvested growth in a tax-deferred annuity is not reported on your tax return. You only report and pay tax on annuity interest when you make a withdrawal. When used properly, these investments can help to lower the taxable portion of you social security income.

WHY DEFER TAX IF YOU HAVE TO PAY IT ANYWAY?

Many investors knowing that they will eventually have to pay the tax, question the value of tax deferred investments. If you defer tax long enough, you may never have to pay it.

Option #1: $100,000 invested for 30 years at a hypothetical 3.72% taxable[68]

Option #2: $100,000 invested for 30 years at a hypothetical 3.72% tax-deferred[69]

At the end of 30 years, the table shows your results.

	Taxable at 3.72%	Tax-Deferred at 3.72% [70]
Year 5	$113,099	$120,036
Year 10	$127,914	$144,087
Year 15	$144,669	$172,957
Year 20	$163,619	$207,611
Year 30	$209,291	$299,141

Would you rather have a nest egg of $299,141 or $209,291? Assume at the end of 30 years, you started to distribute "interest only" from your nest egg. At a 3.72% consistent rate of return your taxable account would provide $7,596 annually or $5,089 after tax. Your tax deferred account would provide you $10,729; $7,596 after tax. That's over $2,000 more each year after taxes from the tax-deferred account. The downside is, your beneficiaries pay the tax when they inherit your tax-deferred account. It may however, make more sense to have higher income during your lifetime. If you don't need the income during your lifetime you could use the difference to purchase a life insurance policy and leave your heirs even more money income and estate tax free.

FIXED IMMEDIATE ANNUITIES

An immediate annuity is a lump sum premium payment to an insurance company in exchange for a monthly income that you cannot outlive.[71] And, each annuity payment is partially tax free.[72]

The amount of money you receive each month is dependent on your age, the amount of your premium, and the term of the payments you select (e.g. lifetime, 10 year period certain, etc…). The older you are when you pay your premium, the higher the monthly payments. The insurance company does not expect to have to make payments as long as they would to a younger person. You may also elect to receive a lower payment in exchange for having the payments continued to your heirs.

A fixed immediate annuity is suitable for someone who:

- is looking to increase their monthly income

- has no heirs or who is not concerned about leaving an estate

- set aside other funds for their heirs.

- is retired, wants a fixed payment and doesn't want to deal with maturing investments, rolling over investments or the maintenance and administration that is required by other investment strategies.

A BETTER ALTERNATIVE TO TAX-FREE BONDS

Tax-free bonds are a popular source of tax-free income for retirees looking to lower their taxes. Many investors however, are not aware that they can potentially receive a much higher tax-free income from an immediate annuity.[73]

Hypothetical Example:

Mr. Jones is 70 years of age with a $500,000 municipal bond portfolio earning a tax-free 4.14%.[74] Each year, his portfolio generates

$20,700 of tax-free income (4.14% x $500,000). If Mr. Jones takes his $500,000 and converts it to an immediate annuity, he will generate $35,050[75] per year of which 74% of the payment is tax-free.[76] He will net $32,043 annually after taxes.[77]   Mr. Jones' spendable income increases by $11,343 annually ($32,043-$20,700).   However, an immediate annuity does not leave anything for his heirs. In Mr. Jones' case, he's quite content with this scenario as he is more interested in his own personal comfort during his lifetime and not how much he leaves in his estate. If he was intent on leaving a large amount of money to his heirs, he may still want to use an immediate annuity, but in a different way.

	Tax-Free Bond	Immediate Annuity
Annual Payment	$20,700	$35,050
Income Tax	0	$3,007
Net to Spend	$20,700	$32,043
Amount Left at Maturity	$500,000	0

Understanding the differences between municipal bonds and immediate annuities:

- Immediate fixed annuities have a stated payout for a stated period of time and municipal bonds have a fixed interest rate for a fixed term.

- Municipal bonds may be callable (cancelled and offered a lower interest rate), while immediate fixed annuities are not.

- The investor pays an upfront commission with municipal bonds, while immediate annuities do not.[78] Municipal bonds may be subject to alternative minimum tax.

- The payments of a fixed immediate annuity are guaranteed by the annuity company. The interest payments of a municipal bond are guaranteed by the issuing municipality.

- A portion of each immediate fixed annuity payment is considered a tax-free return of principal. All municipal bond interest is exempt from federal tax. And in many cases, it is exempt from state tax.

- Immediate fixed annuities are illiquid and cannot be redeemed. Most municipal bonds can be sold at any time on the secondary market at a gain or at a loss. When held to maturity, the issuer guarantees payment of the face value of a municipal bond.

- Immediate annuities provide income for life or the selected term, while municipal bonds provide semi-annual interest until maturity or until they are called.

- At death, a municipal bond is included in the owner's estate. An immediate annuity is not included in the owner's estate at death unless a period certain payout option is selected in which case only the value of all remaining payments would be included.

HEALTH-ADJUSTED SINGLE PREMIUM IMMEDIATE ANNUITIES

Some companies take into account your individual health condition and use that information to calculate your immediate annuity payout. If your health records were to indicate conditions that lowered your life expectancy your monthly payment would increase. However, you would receive this fixed monthly amount no matter how long you live.

Hypothetical Example:

A 70-year-old man deposits $100,000 into a single premium immediate annuity. At a standard 16 year life expectancy, he would receive a monthly payment of $730. However, due to negative health conditions, the annuity company calculates his life expectancy at 10 years and his monthly payment jumps to $1,502.

In the unfortunate event that you have a severe health condition, using a single premium annuity may help to make your remaining years a little easier.

THE SPLIT ANNUITY SOLUTION FOR INCOME AND TAX SAVINGS

Some investors might like the simplicity of an immediate annuity without taking their heirs out of the picture. A split annuity is the combination of a tax-deferred annuity and an immediate annuity. The immediate annuity generates income for a certain number of years. While the immediate annuity is being spent down, the tax-deferred annuity is left to grow. The growth in the tax-deferred annuity is equal to the amount of income paid out by the immediate annuity. By the time the immediate annuity runs out, the tax-deferred annuity has made up the difference. And it's time to start all over again.

Hypothetical Example:

Mrs. Jones has $100,000 to invest. She deposits $76,136 into a fixed deferred annuity earning 5% for six years and the remaining $23,864 into an immediate annuity. The split annuity generates $342 of 96% tax free income for six years. At the end of six years the immediate annuity has been depleted and the deferred annuity is worth $100,000.

Split annuities offer a combination of income, tax savings and capital preservation.

POTENTIAL TAX RELIEF FOR MUTUAL FUND INVESTORS

When you buy individual stocks, you pay no capital gains tax until you sell your shares. This is not the case with mutual funds. Every time the mutual fund manager sells a stock for a gain, you must pay tax on your share of the profit, even if you haven't taken any money. The gain incurred by the fund may be a long-term capital gain or a short-term gain. This is important as short-term capital gains are taxed at rates up to 35% where long-term gains may only be taxed as high as 15%. This tax is in addition to your tax on dividends.

In addition, this tax can be even higher when the market falls. Typically, when the stock market is down, investors get scared and look to sell out of the market. In order to redeem the shares, the fund will often sell holdings to create the cash needed to pay shareholders. Frequently, the sale of these shares will create a tax to the investor. Talk about adding insult to injury.

Many mutual fund managers also manage sub-accounts within variable annuities. In many cases, these sub-accounts contain the same equity holdings as mutual funds. One great aspect of variable annuities is that you do not receive an annual 1099. As you liquidate your variable annuity, you'll be taxed on the gain.[79] Variable annuities can also provide these additional features:[80]

Death Benefit – The insurance company can guarantee a minimum of the initial investment, current value, or they may guarantee a minimum rate of return.

Automatic Account Rebalancing – As different subaccounts within your annuity grow faster than others, your portfolio will change its characteristics, possibly becoming overly conservative or too aggressive (all variable investments such as stocks, bonds, and mutual funds are subject to this). At selected periods of time, some annuities will automatically restructure your investment mix to what it was when you started, selling off the winners (selling high) and reinvesting into the losers (buying low). Whether inside an annuity or not, rebalancing is a critical part of any portfolio.

Guarantee of Principal – Many annuity companies will guarantee your principal as a lump sum or as an income stream at a predetermined date in the future.

Guaranteed Minimum Return – Some annuity companies will promise a minimum rate of return as long as the investor does not surrender their annuity prior to a certain date.

No Upfront Sales Charge – Unlike many mutual funds that require an upfront commission, most variable annuities do not.

Up Front Bonus – Many annuity companies will offer an up front bonus, generally a percentage of the amount invested, as incentive to invest for a longer period of time.

Variable annuities, like any other investment, are not appropriate for every investor. If you are concerned about the uncertainty of the stock market and want to insure that you protect your principal, a variable annuity might be a nice compliment to your portfolio.

PROTECT YOUR PRINCIPAL AND SAVE TAXES

Many investors are willing to sacrifice profit potential for protection of their principal. Countless studies have indicated that the majority of U.S. citizens are less emotionally attached to the prospect of gain than they are to the fear of loss. This can be seen in any casino. Rarely will you see someone bet their mortgage or cash in their entire life's savings for one roll of the dice. Yes, they could make a lot of money, but they could also lose everything they own.

The insurance industry recently introduced the *indexed annuity*. Indexed annuities will give you a portion of the growth in the stock market when the stock market goes up. Typically, it is a percentage of the gain in the S & P 500 index. However, if the stock market goes down, you will receive a predetermined minimum rate of return (typically 2%-3%).[81] By placing this money in the indexed annuity, the original principal is protected.

Indexed annuities are a safe, tax-deferred alternative for CD and money market investors who may have been nervous about placing their money in the stock market.[82] Additionally, this may be an option for people who own annuities that are paying low rates. Many investors saw their fixed annuities go from earning 10% in 1988 to less than 4% now.[83]

Indexed annuities generally do not perform as well as mutual funds or stocks during an increasing stock market, as they provide only a percentage of the increase in the S&P 500, but they may offer a vast improvement over your existing annuity.

Indexed annuities may be well suited for people who want to protect their principal and are concerned that their current investments aren't outpacing the cost of living.

THE OTHER TAX-FREE WAY TO HELP YOUR GRANDCHILDREN

By now you have probably heard of 529 plans as being quite possibly the best way to put away money for children or grandchildren's college expenses. 529 plans are currently exempt from federal tax when distributed to the child to cover qualified education expenses. This exemption is scheduled to expire in 2011. Amounts contributed to a 529 plan on behalf of a child are considered gifts. Amounts contributed in excess of the $11,000 annual gift exclusion would be treated as income to the child. A provision will allow up to 5 years of donations to be made in a single year ($55,000). In addition, these funds count against financial aid benefits at nearly a dollar for dollar basis.

Another option would be to make a tax-free distribution from a variable life insurance policy. The grandparent would take a loan against the policy and use the proceeds to pay tuition. As long as they write the check directly to the educational institution, it is not subject to income or gift taxes.[84] Amounts paid directly to a financial institution that have been distributed from a variable life policy are not considered gifts to the child and are free from gift taxes.[85]

	529 Plans	Variable Life
Choice of investment options	Yes	Yes
Limitation on investment amount	Yes, varies by state	No
Amounts remain in control of donor	Yes	Yes or the donors trust or any other party selected by donor
Included in estate of donor	No	Must be purposely designed to be excluded from estate
Income taxability	Yes to donor plus penalty if donor makes withdrawals	Tax-deferred when withdrawals processed as loans or no tax when proceeds received as death benefit
Income tax to beneficiary	No, tax-free until 2011	No tax if paid directly to financial institution or as a death benefit
Costs	Similar to mutual funds	Similar to mutual funds for the sub-accounts plus mortality and expense charges
Death benefit to child if donor dies before funding complete	No death benefit: child gets account balance	Yes, this is an insurance policy

A grandparent in good health who can qualify for the full (non-rated) amount of insurance may be interested in funding their grandchild's education in this way. If the grandparent were to die before the account is fully funded, the grandchild gets the tax-free death benefit to pay for school.

HOW TO PAY ONLY 5% CAPITAL GAINS TAX

You are probably aware that the long-term capital gains tax rate was cut to 15%, but many investors are unaware that they may be able to qualify for a 5% rate. The 5% capital gains rate applies to taxpayers who are in the 15% marginal income tax bracket. This includes married couples with an income of $56,800 or less and single people with an income of $28,400 or less. While some taxpayers are consistently above these levels, they should not overlook the opportunity to lower their tax bracket for one year in order to take advantage of a lower capital gains rate.

Hypothetical Example:

Mr. & Mrs. Jones have $200,000 worth of AT&T stock. Mr. Jones purchased the stock through an employee stock purchase plan some 20 years ago for a total out of pocket expense of $70,000. Due to the recent purchase of a piece of real estate and an additional mortgage deduction they were able to lower their 28% tax bracket to 15% for this year only. While the 15% regular tax bracket applies to them, they may want to sell their AT&T stock and enjoy paying a 5% tax rate on the $130,000 gain.

Had the Jones' not had a significant tax benefit already they may have wanted to lower their tax bracket on their own using tax-free bond, annuities or a gifting strategy. This may be an opportunity to cut your capital gains taxes by two thirds.

HOW TO SELL REAL ESTATE AND AVOID THE TAX

If you have a single-family rental property that was purchased years ago and now has big gains, you may want to move in. It may not be convenient, but if you and your spouse were to move in and live there for two years, you could then sell and avoid tax on the first $500,000 of growth and if you are single you can exclude the first $250,000 of gain. You could unload a whole portfolio of rental properties potentially tax-free by living in each for two years before selling.

You may own an apartment building that you no longer want to care for. Maybe you have grandchildren across the country and you don't want to think about your apartment building every time you go away to visit them. You could exchange the apartment building for another investment property using a 1031 tax-free exchange.[86] A triple net lease might be an appropriate alternative. Under a triple net lease, the franchisee (i.e. McDonald's or Walgreens) takes total responsibility for the property. Your monthly rent check can be deposited directly into your bank account as you travel to Colorado to visit your grandchildren.

It may be time to get rid of those 500 acres of farm land that don't generate any income. You can donate it to a charitable trust, and as the trustee, sell it tax free. Then you can invest the money as you see fit to receive a hypothetical 8% payout.[87] The tax rules provide flexibility when it comes to real estate. It's easy to harvest profits and avoid taxes in many situations.

Avoiding Tax After The Fact

If you already sold some stock or property and are looking at a big tax bill, it may not be too late to do something about it. While planning before the sale provides a lot more flexibility, there is still a way to save tax after the sale with a gift annuity.

A gift annuity results by making a gift to a qualified charity and you get income from the gift for life. In addition you get an immediate tax deduction that can be used to shelter the tax from your real estate or stock sale.

Hypothetical Example:

Mr. Jones, sells a property for $100,000 that has been fully depreciated. Let's simplify and assume a tax due of $20,000. He shelters this through the use of a gift annuity. He contributes the $100,000 of his proceeds and receives a $6700 annual income for life, of which 43% is considered a tax-free return of principal. In addition, he receives a tax deduction of $29,703 right away. Mr. Jones was able to:

- offset part of his capital gains tax with a $29,703 tax deduction,

- generate a tax efficient lifetime income of $6700 annually,

- benefit his favorite college (The University of Arizona)

Because he does not need the income today, Mr. Jones was able to defer income for 10 years. This increased the amount of income he will receive to $12,400 per year and increased his tax deduction to $55,221. This same technique can be used to shelter taxes from IRA or retirement plan distributions while still providing an annual income.

Chapter Eight

Estate Planning

Investors always want to know the best place to invest money. It's a reasonable question, but it often focuses on the wrong part of the problem. Does it really matter if an investor can get a 3% higher rate of return on their investment, if he or she ignores their estate planning situation and pays the government an unnecessary $500,000? It may make more sense to focus on the best way to preserve the $500,000 rather than how to earn extra $3,000 per year on a $50,000 investment.

Most investors incorrectly believe that estate planning is about giving away their money and losing control of their assets. In fact, estate planning is about maintaining control. If you really want to make a big difference in your financial picture, it may make more sense to focus on estate planning rather than on how to get a higher percentage on your investments, a percentage that the government may get most of anyway.

ESTATE PLANNING FOR THE LESS THAN WEALTHY

The vast majority of people in the United States do not pay estate taxes, yet many will ruin their estate plan. Quite often people will have had an attorney draft a will or trusts years ago thinking they would be good forever, even in the face of a Congress that loves to change the laws.

Additionally, there are other documents that are essential for your estate plan:

*A **durable power of attorney*** – If you become incapacitated due to an injury or illness and are unable to manage your own finances, a durable power of attorney will provide for someone to do this for you. It can take effect immediately or you may choose to have it delayed until a certain action or occurrence takes place (springing power). You specify the required action, such as two doctors declaring you unable to make financial decisions. You can also stipulate the amount of control your *attorney-in-fact* will have over your finances. Without such a document, your bank, securities firm, and the title company will not accept any instructions from your family on your behalf. In fact, the family would be required to go to court and receive a ruling to act on your behalf. This can be an expensive, extremely slow and completely unnecessary process. These powers can include, but are not limited to:

- Paying household expenses

- Handling retirement accounts

- Collecting government benefits

- Filing income tax returns

- Managing a business

- Buying and selling assets

- Making gifts

The person you select to be your attorney-in-fact should be someone you trust and who has shown the ability to manage their own finances competently. This could be a family member, a close friend, an attorney or an accountant. I would encourage you to name an alternate in the case your first selection is unable or unwilling to carry out the tasks when required.

A medical power of attorney – Commonly known as a "healthcare proxy," a "durable power of attorney for health care," or a "medical directive," gives someone else the legal authority to make medical decisions on your behalf if you can no longer make them on your own. As with a "durable power of attorney," I advise you to name an alternate.

A living will – Many people have strong opinions regarding the continuation of life by artificial means or "heroic measures." A living will provides specific instructions to your family explaining under what circumstances you would want to terminate medical support. This document can relieve your loved ones of the responsibility of having to make an extremely difficult choice.

A durable power of attorney, healthcare proxy, and a living will enable you to maintain control of your own destiny and make things much easier on your loved ones.

TRUSTS

When you hear the word "trust" in reference to estate planning, it could mean almost anything. A trust is simply an entity created by placing words on a piece of paper.

That entity becomes a legal being and will often get its own tax ID number and pay taxes like any other taxpayer.

People create trusts because they allow for savings of estate and income taxes, as well as better control over their assets. The different types of trusts are limited only by what you want to accomplish. Here are some of the most common types of trusts:

Living Trusts – The principle benefit of a living trust is that it avoids probate. This trust offers no other substantial benefits such as control or tax savings.

Irrevocable Trust – These trusts are irrevocable and are considered to be outside of your estate. The assets inside this trust do not get included in your estate tax calculation. Irrevocable trusts can be a powerful estate planning tool. Once you place an asset in an irrevocable trust, it will remain exempt from estate taxes no matter how large it gets. These trusts are a popular place to hold life insurance as they offer the ability to make the death benefit income and estate tax-free. The death benefit is exempt from estate tax because it is owned by the trust, not your estate.

Qualified Personal Residence Trust – These trusts allow someone to pass the value of their residence to their heirs at a discounted value. This is popular among homeowners with expensive homes that they want to shelter from estate taxes. You may continue to live in your house for the term of the trust which you select. At the end of the term, the house passes out of your estate to the QPRT at a discounted value. You may then want to rent it back from your heirs and continue to live there.

Grantor Retained Income Trust – Similar to the "Residence Trust" above, this trust enables you to place assets such as stocks, bonds, or investment real estate into the trust. You receive an income stream for a specified number of years, after which the assets pass to your beneficiaries at a discounted value.

2503c Trusts – These trusts hold assets for minors. Unlike the "Uniform Gift to Minors Trust" with which many parents are familiar, this type of trust allows you to place restrictions on the assets (i.e. assets remain in the trust until the child reaches a certain age or finishes college etc.).

Understanding how a trust can benefit your situation may provide the incentive you need to start doing something about your estate planning situation.

DISCLAIMER

People will often delay their estate planning because they are not exactly certain what they want to accomplish. Somewhat understandably, they would rather risk paying excess taxes and subjecting their children to the probate system, than hurry into a bad decision. In such cases, having your beneficiaries know about a disclaimer may be beneficial.

Hypothetical Example:

Mr. Jones has a son who is doing extremely well financially as a physician. Mr. Jones would like his son to be the beneficiary of his estate when he dies. However, his son is well on his way to growing his own significant estate and having similar problems with which to deal. If he were to leave additional assets to his son, he would be compounding his son's estate planning problem by making it more difficult to pass assets onto to his children (Mr. Jones' grandchildren). But, Mr. Jones does not want to leave assets directly to his grandchildren.

By way of a disclaimer, Mr. Jones can leave the assets to his son. However, if at the time of inheritance the son would rather have the assets go directly to his children, he can disclaim the inheritance. The assets never become part of the son's estate when the disclaimer is used and the inheritance is treated as if it passes from the grandparent to the grandchild.[88]

The disclaimer provides great flexibility in estate planning. The disclaimer could direct the assets to a charity if the recipient so desires and the estate plan is so constructed. With planning and knowledge of the disclaimer, some very accommodating estate plans can be assembled.

MISTAKES WITH YOUR LIVING TRUST

Many people do the right thing by having a living trust prepared. A living trust prevents your heirs from being subjected to the lengthy, costly and needless probate process. These same trustees often fail to investigate how to make the most of their living trust. Once the trust is completed you may still have work to do. In fact, many people make errors that can be extremely costly:

Leaving assets outright to your heirs – Over the past few years the focus of many investors has changed from simply protecting their estate from taxes to a concern as to how the money is used. The majority of trusts I see leave assets outright to heirs. The heirs are free to squander the assets while their creditors are free to attach these assets. Many people have included instructions in their trusts that determine how the assets are distributed to their heirs when they die. By including these directives, their assets may be better protected from outside forces.

A growing number of people have begun expressing concern over the work ethic of their child's generation. They are worried that leaving their children a substantial amount of money may not provide incentive for their children to work hard and become meaningful members of society. It is a frequently observed phenomenon that rather than adding to the wealth created by the parents, the next generation typically dissipates it.

I suggest a simple process whereby the assets in your living trust are placed in a bypass trust at your death. The bypass trust continues at least throughout the lives of your children. The income from the trust can be distributed to your heirs using the precise instructions you left for them regarding how and when the principal can be distributed (e.g. to buy a house, to start a business etc...). While assets remain in this bypass trust they enjoy protection from creditors as well as family disputes. In an age where divorce rates are the highest they have ever been, a bypass trust prevents an ex son-in-law or daughter-in-law from having claim to these assets.

Failure to manage the bypass trust correctly - When one spouse dies, a bypass trust is created and funded with the assets of the deceased spouse. Many people put little thought as to which to place in the bypass trust and how they should be managed. Selecting the right assets is very important for wealth creation and tax reasons. Assets in the bypass trust should have two objectives:

1. Grow as much as possible

2. Generate zero taxes.

These are two very clear cut objectives, yet these assets are frequently managed incorrectly for the following reason:

The surviving spouse invests the bypass trust assets to generate income for their own benefit - At the same time, their own assets are growing in value and become subject to estate taxes. The surviving spouse would be better to spend down his or her own assets to ensure that those assets remain below the estate taxable level, while allowing the bypass trust to grow as much as possible. One of the best uses of a bypass trust is as an irrevocable life insurance trust. Such an arrangement can pay a larger sum to your heirs and is completely tax-free.

Hypothetical Example:

The assets in a bypass trust are used to purchase a life insurance policy that is scheduled to pay out when the second parent dies. Heirs receive 200% to 600% of the premium invested income and estate tax-free.

Selecting the wrong successor trustee – Many parents select one or all of their children as successor trustee(s). This can be a formula for disaster, creating hard feelings and misunderstandings among siblings, and even costly mistakes if the children are not business savvy. I generally encourage people to select an independent trustee who is knowledgeable in estate matters and can settle an estate efficiently.

Just having a living trust may not be enough. Take the time to ensure that it will be effective when you need it.

AVOIDING PROBATE WITHOUT A LIVING TRUST

Probate is the court process which divides your estate based on your will or State law. In an effort to avoid probate, some people will title their assets in joint tenancy. Joint tenancy will avoid probate, but it may create other problems. Joint tenancy can create a gift that must be reported on a gift tax return. More importantly, you expose the asset to the legal liabilities of the other party.

Hypothetical Example:

You own a piece of investment real estate jointly with your son. Your son is a general contractor and is involved with a building where someone gets severely injured. The injured man sues your son and attaches his assets of which you are part owner. The asset you own in joint tenancy with your son is placed at risk.

As previously discussed, a living trust which also avoids probate will not expose your assets to any other's liability. Additionally, be aware of how your will deals with estate taxes. If the taxes are to be divided equally among your 3 children, all may pay tax on a real estate investment that only one child will inherit.

LIFE AFTER DEATH TAXES

Over the years, the death tax has been a tug of war battle. One group of politicians wants to keep the tax to "soak the rich" while another fights to abolish it because of the hardship it places on certain people. Regardless of where you stand on the issue, one thing is certain: even if the federal estate tax is permanently repealed, a tax in one form or another will replace it. If you do not remain flexible and take appropriate action, you or your heirs will pay.

The estate tax exemption is scheduled to increase each year through 2009, and then is repealed for 1 year in 2010 (scheduled to come back in 2011). The death tax brings in about $24 billion each year to the federal government, and when it is phased out in 2010, more money might actually flow in the IRS coffers. That's because the step-up in basis for inherited property is phasing out as well.

The way that the capital gains tax on inherited property currently works is that your heirs receive your assets at the market value on the date of your death.[89] If they sell the assets for that amount, they avoid the capital gains tax, and any appreciation above the date-of-death value is taxable (as a capital gain). Under the phase out legislation, assets would begin to be inherited at their purchase price rather than market value (carryover basis), and heirs would inherit old capital-gains tax liabilities. Estates would escape the death tax but heirs could owe capital gains tax based on the original purchase of the property. This could encourage people to sell assets during their lifetime, pay the capital gains tax, and reinvest the proceeds. Tax revenue to the government would be generated sooner.

And, if the carryover basis were maintained after 2010, when the estate tax is automatically reinstated, your heirs could end up brutally taxed on both the value of inherited assets as well as old gains on those assets.

Let us not forget about the states and their combined, projected $57.9 billion deficit for 2003.[90] Presently, they get a federal credit that is scheduled to phase out from 2003 to 2007. This could cost the states a collective $23 billion in revenues. Some states have already taken action to defend their interests. Seventeen states (including Massachusetts) and the District of Columbia have "decoupled" relevant parts of their tax code from changes in the federal tax code to keep it as it was prior to the 2001 federal estate tax law amendments.

Now is not the time to become complacent. Now is the time to implement strategies that could possibly save you tax dollars today and your heirs' money in the future.

ARE YOU WORTH MORE THAN THE AMOUNT OF YOUR EXEMPTION?

Everyone who defines themselves as "middle income or higher" should be conscious of estate taxes. Every dollar you have over the current exemption amount ($1.5 million in 2005) at death will be taxed up to 48%. With a rising stock market and increasing home values more people than ever are exceeding the amount of their exemption. If you are only slightly above this threshold (e.g. you have an estate of $1.7 million in 2005), then a gifting strategy should suffice to gift excess estate values to your beneficiaries by way of a living trust.

If you are a substantially over the current exemption amount ($1.5 million in 2005), your estate is probably growing faster than a gifting strategy will enable you to reduce your estate. Currently non-taxable gifts are limited to $11,000 per year per grantor per recipient. Rather than waiting until you die to use your exemption, you may want to use it now.

Hypothetical Example:

Mr. Smith is 65 years of age and has stock which is equal in value to the current estate tax exemption amount that he plans on leaving to his estate. If he were to gift it today, he can use his exemption and give it away tax free. If he waits, the stock could double in value over the next ten years and then he would have an even bigger estate tax problem.

You may be reluctant to give up control of the stock through a gift and you do not need to give up control. The gift can be made in the form of a trust, which you or your spouse can tap into if needed, or you can continue to control the stock through a family limited partnership and continue to receive income (in the form of management fees or loans).

How Your Family Limited Partnership Can Save You Big Tax Dollars

For years, the wealthy have been using estate planning techniques that may be unfamiliar to most but could benefit many. One such technique is the "Family Limited Partnership."

Hypothetical Example:

Mr. and Mrs. Jones own a farm valued at $1 million. If it is left in their estate, this property could be burdened with estate taxes up to 48% of the value. Using a family limited partnership they can "shrink" the value of their estate for estate tax purposes. The farm gets deeded to the family partnership in a non-taxable event. In return for donating the farm to their family partnership, the Jones' receive 100 partnership "units" (shares) as evidence of their ownership in the partnership. Each year, they begin gifting some of these partnership units to their children. You might think that each unit is worth $10,000 ($1 million divided by 100 units). For estate tax purposes, the farm inside the family partnership is worth less. Each partnership unit is worth only $7,000 (for tax purposes) in the hands of your children. The discounted value is ascertained by an appraiser who is experienced in setting discounts for family partnership assets. The IRS allows a valuation discount for two reasons:

1. *Lack of Marketability* – The IRS agrees that the units they gift to their children are virtually unsellable to anyone.

2. *Minority Interest* – Their children have no control over the farm. This is called the "minority interest" discount. As a result, the farm value for estate tax purposes is only $700,000. They have just wiped out $300,000 of estate value for a potential estate tax savings of $144,000 by forming a family limited partnership.

Even though over time the partnership units are gifted away to their children (to remove the value from your estate), the Jones' remain the lifetime general partner. That means they are always in control. They decide how the farm gets managed, whether to sell it or borrow against it or whatever decisions are made. Additionally, the assets in the partnership are protected from law suits and creditors. For a combination of estate tax savings, protection from creditors and ease of estate distribution, a family partnership can be a very powerful tool.

WHERE WILL YOUR HEIRS COME UP WITH THE MONEY?

It is well known that when you die you can leave an unlimited amount of wealth to your spouse without paying estate tax. The problem arises when your surviving spouse dies. With taxes up to 48%, your assets are included in his or her taxable estate. Payment of estate taxes is due in nine months and in cash. Often, heirs are forced to liquidate the family homestead or other personal assets to pay the estate tax, while IRAs lose over a third of their value to income tax. Purchasing a life insurance policy to cover these costs may be an alternative.

Second-to-die life insurance, also known as "survivorship life," insures two lives. The payout occurs at the death of the second insured. Typically, the beneficiaries will use the death proceeds to provide the liquidity needed to pay estate taxes (federal & state), income tax, and other settlement costs.

The premiums for second-to-die life insurance may be less than a standard life policy, particularly if you or your spouse is not healthy. Insurance companies determine rates based on your projected life expectancy. With second-to-die policies, the company will put greater weight on the healthier of the two since they will not have to payout a benefit until the second death. Even if you or your spouse has a serious medical problem that would cause a standard policy to be rated or declined, a second-to-die policy may be obtainable.

Second-to-die life insurance is generally for couples with taxable estates over $1.5 million. Now, you may think such a figure does not apply to you. However, escalating real estate prices, several decades of an expanding stock market, and plain old inflation have pushed many middle-class Americans above the $1.5 million mark.

Estate taxes are scheduled to phase out by 2010, and unless Congress takes action, in 2011 couples with taxable estates of $1,000,000 or more will be looking at a potential 55% estate tax. Additionally, many states are modifying their own estate tax laws. Whether there will be further changes has been the subject of much speculation and debate. But, do you really want to bet a substantial portion of your estate on the whims' of politicians? If you are concerned about taxes eroding your estate, some insurance companies have introduced an option that may be of interest to you.

> *Estate tax repeal rider* – This rider will allow you to terminate a policy without paying surrender charges as long as the estate tax is fully repealed in 2010. You keep the protection if the tax remains, or you can choose to get your money back if the tax is abolished, and the insurance is no longer needed.

Second-to-die life insurance policies are popular investments for people who want to create cash to pay estate taxes. The plans pay when the surviving spouse dies, and if structured properly, the benefits are kept out of the couple's estate. Quite often, a second-to-die policy is less expensive and easier to obtain than two individual policies. If uncertainty about the federal estate tax has kept you from protecting your assets, a second-to-die policy with the "estate tax repeal rider" may be the right thing for you.

NEVER OWN LIFE INSURANCE

Owning life insurance is a big mistake. It is fine to have life insurance to protect your family or for payment of estate taxes, but you never want to own it. Your life insurance policy should be owned outside of your estate.

Your life policy has a surrender value (the amount you get if you cash it in) and a death benefit (the amount the beneficiary gets when you die). Even though the surrender value is the real value to you, the IRS will levy estate tax on the entire death benefit if this policy remains in your name (your estate).

How do you get a policy out of your estate? You can gift it to your children or to an irrevocable trust that you establish for the benefit of your children. If the cash value is less than the estate exemption amount then there is no tax when you make the gift. If the amount of the cash value exceeds your $11,000 annual exclusion ($22,000, if married) you will use up some of your estate tax exemption. In addition, the IRS will pull the death benefit back into your estate if you die within three years of gifting a policy. Some people may even make the gift and then buy a three-year term policy to pay the estate taxes on the policy if they die within the three-year window.

In an effort to avoid the 3 year look back period, many people will consider selling the life policy to their children. This will work. However, the IRS has set up another trap. The policy is exposed to the "transfer for value" rule. When the eventual death benefits are paid to the children, they will be taxable (normally, death benefits are tax free).[91]

If you own life insurance and your estate exceeds the current exemption amount, you should consider removing the policy from you estate.

How Not To Own Long-Term Care
Insurance

Your need for traditional estate planning may be overshadowed by the scheduled phase out of the death tax in 2010. With a projected $450 billion federal budget deficit in 2004, it is debatable whether the estate tax will die. The costs for long-term care are on the rise, and so is your chance of needing it. You may want to look at a strategy that can provide for the costs of long-term care and remove assets from your estate, should the estate tax stay with us.

Hypothetical Example:

Mr. Smith makes a gift to his daughter who then purchases a long-term care insurance policy on him with a "return of premium at death" option. Each year, Mr. Smith will make these gifts to his daughter, who would then pay the annual premiums. When Mr. Smith dies, his daughter would receive a death benefit for the total of all premiums paid less any long-term care benefits. Because the policy was not included in his estate, the daughter would receive the death benefit estate tax free.

Having an appropriate long-term care plan can help provide for your needs, ensure sufficient income for your spouse, and preserve assets for your beneficiaries.

How To Leverage Your Annuity

If you own stocks or mutual funds, there is a good chance that the values are less than they were a few years ago. Your choice is either to sell them or to hold onto them. If you have a variable annuity you may have a third option that could benefit your heirs.

Most annuity companies promise to pay your beneficiaries at least the amount you invested in the contract, even if it is greater than the contract's value on the day of your death. Some issuers also offer a death benefit that goes up each year by a specified percentage or with the highest contract anniversary value.

Hypothetical Example:

Mr. Johnson invested $100,000 in a variable annuity with an escalating death benefit tied to anniversary dates. At the 3rd contract anniversary, the account was valued at $125,000. The contract is currently worth $75,000. Mr. Johnson's heirs are guaranteed to receive at least $125,000. There is however a way to possibly increase that amount.

Mr. Johnson may want to obtain another annuity contract. A 1031 tax-free, partial exchange from one annuity to another may allow him to lock in some of the death benefit on the first contract and get an additional death benefit with a second. If Mr. Johnson removed $70,000 from the original contract, he would still have $55,000 in life insurance ($125,000 less $70,000). He could then invest the $70,000 into a second annuity, which includes a $70,000 death benefit.

If both annuities grow by 6% per year for five years, the death benefit for the first annuity would remain at $55,000. However, the second annuity's cash value and death benefit will have increased to $93,676, and Mr. Johnson's beneficiaries would receive $148,676. That's

$23,676 more than if he had left the money in a single account.

This concept may not work for all individuals and might not be allowed with some annuity contracts, and surrender charges and other restrictions need to be considered. Nevertheless, it could possibly be an ideal method to substantially increase the amount of money to your heirs.

ETHICAL WILLS

When most people think about estate planning they envision trusts, trustees, executors, lawyers, and all of the other complications associated with providing for loved-ones. This is of course necessary and often takes a team of experts to have it done right. There is something that you can do on your own, modify whenever you wish, and will outlast the largest estate.

An ethical will is a piece of you that is a kind of farewell letter, a legacy of your life. You can make it as short or as long as you wish. It is a way for you to tell your family and future generations how you feel about life, your experiences, the decisions you have made, and the moral standards you hope they will inherit from you.

There is no right or wrong way to start. You can begin with something that happened today or go back to your childhood. Just let it come from the heart and the words will flow. You could include stories about your ancestors, people or events that shaped your life, previously untold tales or things that you did which you now regret. It does not need to be in writing. You could record it on a simple tape player or in front of a video camera.

Besides offering guidance to your heirs, an ethical will may help you come to terms with your own mortality. It is a way of creating something of meaning that you wish to pass on and will survive long after you are gone. Upon completion of your ethical will, you need to make sure someone knows about it. You should tell a close friend, your attorney, or trusted family member where it is, who should receive it, and when they should read it.

Glossary

1035 exchange   Section 1035 sets out provisions for the exchange of similar (insurance related) assets without any tax consequence upon the conversion. If the exchange qualifies for like-kind exchange consideration, income taxes are deferred until the new property or asset is sold. The 1035 exchange provisions are only available for a limited type of asset which includes cash value life insurance policies and annuity contracts.

401(k) plan   A 401(k) plan is a tax-deferred defined contribution retirement plan that gives eligible employees the opportunity to defer a portion of their current compensation into the plan. Amounts that are deferred are excluded from the participant's gross income for the year of the deferral. The plan may provide for employer matching contributions and discretionary profit-sharing contributions.

403(b) plan   Tax deferred annuity retirement plan available to employees of public schools and colleges, and certain non-profit hospitals, charitable, religious, scientific and educational organizations.

457 plan   Non-qualified deferred compensation plans available to employees of state and local governments and tax-exempt organizations.

accidental death benefit   An accidental death benefit is a rider added to an insurance policy which provides that an additional death benefit will be paid in the event death is caused by and accident. This rider is often called "double indemnity."

amortization   The amortization of a debt is its systematic repayment through installments of principal and interest. An amortization schedule is a periodic table illustrating payments, principal, interest, and outstanding balance.

annuitant   An individual who receives payments from an annuity. The person whose life the annuity payments are measured on or determined by.

annuity   A contract between an insurance company and an individual which generally guarantees lifetime income to the individual or whose life the contract is based in return for either a lump sum or periodic payment to the insurance company. Interest earned inside an annuity is income tax-deferred until it is paid out or withdrawn.

basis   An amount usually representing the actual cost of an investment to the buyer. The basis amount of an investment is important in calculating capital gains and losses, depreciation, and other income tax calculations.

beneficiary   The person who is designated to receive the benefits of a contract.

beta   A statistically generated number that is used to measure the volatility of a security or mutual fund in comparison to the market as a whole.

blue-chip stocks   The equity issues of financially stable, well-established companies that usually have a history of being able to pay dividends in bear and bull markets.

bond   A certificate of indebtedness issued by a government entity or a corporation, which pays a fixed cash coupon at regular intervals. The coupon payment is normally a fixed percentage of the initial investment. The face value of the bond is repaid to the investor upon maturity.

buy-sell agreement   An agreement between shareholders or business partners to purchase each others' shares in specified circumstances.

cash value   Permanent life insurance policies provide both a death benefit and in an investment component called a cash value. The cash value earns interest and often appreciates. The policyholder may accumulate significant cash value over the years and, in some circumstances, "borrow" the appreciated funds without paying taxes on the borrowed gains. As long as the policy stays in force the borrowed funds do not need to be repaid, but interest may be charged to your cash value account.

certificate of deposit (cd)   A Certificate of Deposit is a low risk, often federally guaranteed investment offered by banks. A CD pays interest to investors for as long as five years. The interest rate on a CD is fixed for the duration of the CD term.

charitable remainder trust (crt)   The Charitable Remainder Trust is an irrevocable trust with both charitable and non-charitable beneficiaries. The donor transfers highly appreciated assets into the trust and retains an income interest. Upon expiration of the income interest, the remainder in the trust passes to a qualified charity of the donor's choice. If properly structured, the CRT permits the donor to receive income, estate, and/or gift tax advantages. These advantages often provide for a much greater income stream to the income beneficiary than would be available outside the trust.

closed-end fund   A fund whose value is held within a fixed number of shares. Until the fund is wound up, shares can be bought and sold on the stock exchange or the over-the-counter market.

commodity   A commodity is a physical substance such as a food or a metal which investors buy or sell on a commodities exchange, usually via futures contracts.

compounding   The computation of interest paid using the principal plus the previously earned interest.

conduit ira   An individual who rolled over a total distribution from a qualified plan into an IRA can later roll over those assets into a new employer's plan. In this case the IRA has been used as a holding account (a conduit).

convertible term insurance   Term life insurance that can be converted to a permanent or whole life policy without evidence of insurability, subject to time limitations.

coupon rate   The rate of interest paid on a bond, expressed as a percentage of the bond's par value.

currency risk   The level of risk when investing in international markets, due to the fluctuations in exchange rates of the various world currencies. Investing in any foreign country should be preceded by a careful estimation of how well its currency is likely to do against the dollar.

custodian   A financial institution, usually a bank or trust company, that holds a person or company's cash and or securities in safekeeping.

debt to income ratio   The ratio of a person's total monthly debt obligations compared to their total monthly resources is called their debt to income ratio. This ratio is used to evaluate a borrower's capacity to repay debts.

decedent   The term decedent refers to a person who has died.

deferral   A form of tax sheltering in which all earnings arc allowcd to compound tax-free until they are withdrawn at a future date. Placing funds in a qualified plan, for example, triggers deductions [not all qualified plans provide for tax deductions; contributions may, however, be excluded from gross income, i.e. 401(k) plans] for the current tax year and postpones capital gains or other income taxes until the funds are withdrawn from the plan.

deferred compensation   Income withheld by an employer and paid at some future time, usually upon retirement or termination of employment.

defined benefit plan   A defined benefit plan pays participants a specific retirement benefit that is promised (defined) in the plan document. Under a defined benefit plan benefits must be definitely determinable. For example, a plan that entitles a participant to a monthly pension benefit for life equal to 30 percent of monthly compensation is a defined benefit plan.

defined contribution plan   In a defined contribution plan, contributions are allocated to individual accounts according to a pre-determined contribution allocation. This type of plan does not promise any specific dollar benefit to a participant at retirement. Benefits received are based on amounts contributed, investment performance and vesting. The most common type of defined contribution plan is the 401(k) profit-sharing plan.

deflation   A period in which the general price level of goods and services is declining.

depreciation   Charges made against earnings to write off the cost of a fixed asset over its estimated useful life. Depreciation does not represent a cash outlay. It is a bookkeeping entry representing the decline in value of an asset over time.

disability insurance   Insurance designed to replace a percentage of earned income if accident or illness prevents the beneficiary from pursuing his or her livelihood.

diversification   Spreading investment risk among a number of different securities, properties, companies, industries or geographical locations. Diversification does not assure against market loss.

dividend reinvestment plan (drip)   An investment plan that allows shareholders to receive stock in lieu of cash dividends.

dividends   A distribution of the earnings of a company to it's shareholders. Dividends are "declared" by the company based on profitability and can change from time to time. There is a direct relationship between dividends paid and share value growth. The most aggressive growth companies do not pay a dividend, and the highest dividend paying companies may not experience dramatic growth.

dollar cost averaging   Buying a mutual fund or securities using a consistent dollar amount of money each month (or other period). More securities will be bought when prices are low, resulting in lowering the average cost per share. *Dollar cost averaging neither guarantees a profit nor eliminates the risk of losses in declining markets and* *you should consider your ability to continue investing through periods of market volatility and/or low prices.*

earnings per share (eps)   Total net profits divided by the number of outstanding common shares of a company.

employee stock ownership plans (esops)   An ESOP plan allows employees to purchase stock, usually at a discount, that they can hold or sell. ESOPs offer a tax advantage for both employer and employee. The employer earns a tax deduction for contributions of stock or cash used to purchase stock for the employee. The employee pays no tax on these contributions until they are distributed.

executor   The person named in a will to manage the estate of the deceased according to the terms of the will.

face amount   The face amount stated in a life insurance policy is the amount that will be paid upon death, or policy maturity. The face amount of a permanent insurance policy may change with time as the cash value in the policy increases.

family trust   An inter vivos trust established with family members as beneficiaries.

federal national mortgage association (fnma or fannie mae)   FNMA is a private corporation that acts as a secondary market investor in buying and selling mortgage loans.

fiduciary   An individual or institution occupying a position of trust. An executor, administrator or trustee.

guarantor   A third party who agrees to repay any outstanding balance on a loan if you fail to do so. A guarantor is responsible for the debt only if the principal debtor defaults on the loan.

home equity line of credit (heloc)   A home equity line of credit allows a homeowner to borrow against the equity in their home with specific limits and terms. This is an open end loan which allows the borrower to borrow and repay funds as needed.

home equity loan   A home equity loan is a collateralized mortgage, usually in a subordinate position, entered into by the property owner under specific terms of repayment.

illiquid   The description of a security for which it is difficult to find a buyer or seller. An illiquid investment is an investment that may be difficult to sell quickly at a price close to its market value. Examples include stock in private unlisted companies, commercial real estate and limited partnerships.

inflation   A term used to describe the economic environment of rising prices and declining purchasing power.

in-force policy   An in-force life insurance policy is simply a valid policy. Generally speaking, a life insurance policy will remain in-force as long as sufficient premiums are paid, and for approximately 31 days thereafter.

insurability   Insurability refers to the assessment of the applicant's health and is used to gauge the level of risk the insurer would potentially take by underwriting a policy, and therefore the premium it must charge.

insured   A life insurance policy covers the life of one or more insured individuals.

interest rate   The simple interest rate attached to the terms of a mortgage or other loan. This rate is applied to the outstanding principal owed in determining the portion of a payment attributable to interest and to principal in any given payment.

interest rate risk   Is the uncertainty in the direction of interest rates. Changes in interest rates could lead to capital loss, or a yield less than that available to other investors, putting at risk the earnings capacity of capital.

intestate   A term describing the legal status of a person who dies without a will.

ira (individual retirement account)   An Individual Retirement Account (IRA) is a personal savings plan that offers tax advantages to those who set aside money for retirement. Depending on the individual's circumstances, contributions to the IRA may be deductible in whole or in part. Generally, amounts in an IRA, including earnings and gains, are not taxed until distributed to the individual.

ira rollover   An individual may withdraw, tax-free, all or part of the assets from one IRA, and reinvest them within 60 days in another IRA. A rollover of this type can occur only once in any one-year period. The one-year rule applies separately to each IRA the individual owns. An individual must roll over into another IRA the same property he/she received from the old IRA.

junk bonds   A bond that pays an unusually higher rate of return to compensate for a low credit rating.

keogh   A Keogh is a tax deferred retirement plan for self-employed individuals and employees of unincorporated businesses. A Keogh plan is similar to an IRA but with significantly higher contribution limits.

leverage   Using "leverage" is the process of investing using borrowed funds. Leveraging your investments magnifies your returns, both positive and negative.

lien   A lien represents a claim against a property or asset for the payment of a debt. Examples include a mortgage, a tax lien, a court judgment, etc.

life insurance   A contract between you and a life insurance company that specifies that the insurer will provide either a stated sum or a periodic income to your designated beneficiaries upon your death.

life settlement   Occurs when a person who does not have a terminal or chronic illness sells his/her life insurance policy to a third party for an amount that is less than the full amount of the death benefit. The buyer becomes the new owner and/or beneficiary of the life insurance policy, pays all future premiums, and collects the entire death benefit when the insured dies. Some states regulate the purchase as a security while others may regulate it as insurance.

liquidity   Liquidity is the measure of your ability to immediately turn assets into cash without penalty or risk of loss. Examples include a savings account, money market account, checking account, etc.

living will   If you become incapacitated this document will preserve your wishes and act as your voice in medical decisions, if you are unable to speak for yourself as a result of medical reasons.

margin   The amount of money supplied by an investor as a portion of the total funds needed to buy or sell a security, with the balance of required funds loaned to the investor by a broker, dealer, or other lender.

medical power of attorney   This special power of attorney document allows you to designate another person to make medical decisions on your behalf.

minimum distributions   An individual must start receiving distributions from a qualified plan by April 1 of the year following the year in which he/she reaches age 70 ½ . Subsequent distributions must occur by each December 31st. The minimum distributions can be based on the life expectancy of the individual or the joint life expectancy of the individual and beneficiary.

money purchase plan   A Money Purchase Plan has contributions that are a fixed percentage of compensation and are not based on the employer's profits. For example, if the plan requires that contributions be 10% of the participant's compensation, the plan is a Money Purchase Pension Plan. With this type of plan, the employer is committed to making contributions each year even if the employer has no profits or is experiencing cash flow problems. Employee contributions are limited to 25% of compensation. Employer contributions are limited to the smaller of $30,000 or 25 percent of a participant's compensation.

mortality   Mortality is the risk of death of a given person based on factors such as age, health, gender, and lifestyle.

municipal bonds   A bond offered by a state, county, city or other political entity (such as a school district) to raise public funds for special projects. The interest received from municipal bonds is often exempt from certain income taxes.

mutual funds   A mutual fund is a pooling of investor (shareholder) assets, which is professionally managed by an investment company for the benefit of the fund's shareholders. Each fund has specific investment objectives and associated risk. Mutual funds offer shareholders the advantage of diversification and professional management in exchange for a management fee.

net asset value   The value of all the holdings of a mutual fund, less the fund's liabilities [also describes the price at which fund shares are redeemed].

net worth   Your net worth is the difference between your total assets and total liabilities.

note   A note is a legal document that acknowledges a debt and the terms and conditions agreed upon by the borrower.

open-end fund   An open-end mutual fund continuously issues and redeems units, so the number of units outstanding varies from day to day. Most mutual funds are open-end funds. The opposite of a closed-end fund.

over-the-counter (otc) market   Market created by dealer trading as opposed to the auction market, which prevails on most major exchanges.

power of attorney   A legal document authorizing one person to act on behalf of another.

premium   The payment that the owner of a life insurance policy makes to the insurer. In exchange for the premium payment, the insurer assumes the financial risk (as defined by the insurance policy) associated with the death of the insured.

probate   The process used to make an orderly distribution and transfer of property from the deceased to a group of beneficiaries. The probate process is characterized by court supervision of property transfer, filing of claims against the estate by creditors and publication of a last will and testament.

profit sharing plan   A Profit-Sharing Plan is the most flexible and simplest of the defined contribution plans. It permits discretionary annual contributions that are generally allocated on the basis of compensation. The employer will determine the amount to be contributed each year depending on the cash-flow of the company. The deduction for contributions to a Profit-Sharing Plan cannot be more than 15% of the compensation paid to the employees participating in the plan. Annual employer contributions to the account of a participant cannot exceed the smaller of $30,000 or 25 percent of a participant's compensation.

prospectus   A detailed statement prepared by an issuer and filed with the SEC prior to the sale of a new issue. The prospectus gives detailed information on the issue and on the issuer's condition and prospects.

qualified retirement plan   A qualified retirement plan is a retirement plan that meets certain specified tax rules contained primarily in section 401(a) of the Internal Revenue Code. These rules are called "plan qualification rules". If the rules are satisfied the plan's trust is exempt from taxes.

rider   A life insurance rider is an amendment to the standard policy that expands or restricts the policy's benefits. Common riders include a disability waiver of premium rider and a children's life coverage rider.

risk   Investment risk is the chance that the actual returns realized on an investment will differ from the expected return.

salary reduction simplified employee pension (sarsep)
A SARSEP is a simplified alternative to a 401(k) plan. It is a SEP that includes a salary reduction arrangement. Under this special arrangement, eligible employees can elect to have the employer contribute part of their before-tax pay to their IRA. This amount is called an "elective deferral."

sec   The main regulatory body regulating the securities industry is called the Securities and Exchange Commission.

simplified employee pension (sep)   A SEP provides employers with a "simplified" alternative to a qualified profit-sharing plan. Basically, a SEP is a written arrangement that allows an employer to make contributions towards his or her own and employees' retirement, without becoming involved in a more complex retirement plan. Under a SEP, IRAs are set up for each eligible employee. SEP contributions are made to IRAs of the participants in the plan. The employer has no control over the employee's IRA once the money is contributed.

small cap   A small cap stock is one issued by a company with less than $1.7 billion in market capitalization.

spousal ira   An individual can set up and contribute to an IRA for his/her spouse. This is called a "Spousal IRA" and can be established if certain requirements are met. In the case of a spousal IRA, the individual and spouse must have separate IRAs. A jointly owned IRA is not permitted.

stop-loss order   This is when you tell your broker to sell the stock if it drops to a certain price.

surrender value   When a policy owner surrenders his/her permanent life insurance policy to the insurance company, he or she will receive the surrender value of that policy in return. The surrender value is the cash value of the policy plus any dividend accumulations, plus the cash value of any paid-up additions minus any policy loans, interest, and applicable surrender charges.

tax credit   An income tax credit directly reduces the amount of income tax paid by offsetting other income tax liabilities.

tax deduction   A reduction of total income before the amount of income tax payable is calculated.

tax-deferred   The term tax deferred refers to the deferral of income taxes on interest earnings until the interest is withdrawn form the investment. Some vehicles or products that enjoy this special tax treatment include permanent life insurance, annuities, and any investment held in IRA's.

tenants in common   Two or more people who own the same piece of property, with the inherent condition that if one of the tenants die, his interest automatically passes on to his heirs.

term insurance   Term insurance is life insurance coverage that pays a death benefit only if the insured dies within a specified period of time. Term policies do not have a cash value component and must be renewed periodically as dictated by the insurance contract.

testamentary trust   A trust created under the terms of a will and that takes effect upon the death of the testator.

top-heavy plans   Each year, a qualified plan must be tested to determine whether it is "top-heavy". Generally, a "top-heavy" plan is one in which more than 60 percent of the benefits under the plan are for key employees (usually owners and officers). Additional requirements apply to a top-heavy plan such as faster vesting and mandatory employer contributions.

total disability   In order to make a disability claim a person must meet the definition of disability set forth in the insurance contract. There are two general definitions of disability used in today's contracts. The first definition is that the insured is unable to perform all of the substantial and material duties of his/her own occupation. The second, and more restrictive, definition is that the insured is unable to perform any occupation for which he/she is reasonably suited by education, training, or experience.

treasury bill   Treasury bills, often referred to as T-bills, are short-term securities (maturities of less than one year) offered and guaranteed by the federal government. They are issued at a discount and pay their full face value at maturity.

treasury bond   Treasury bonds are issued with maturities of more than 10 years and are offered and guaranteed by the U.S. Government. They are issued at a discount and pay their full face value at maturity.

treasury note   Treasury notes are issued with maturities between one and 10 years. These notes are offered and guaranteed by the U.S. Government. They are issued at a discount and pay their full face value at maturity.

tsa (tax-sheltered annuity)   Tax deferred annuity retirement plan available to employees of public schools and colleges, and certain non-profit hospitals, charitable, religious, scientific and educational organizations.

underwriter (insurance)   The one assuming a risk in return for the payment of a premium, or the person who assesses the risk and establishes premium rates.

universal life insurance   An adjustable Universal Life insurance policy provides both a death benefit and an investment component called a cash value. The cash value earns interest at rates dictated by the insurer. The policyholder may accumulate significant cash value over the years and, in some circumstances, "borrow" the appreciated funds without paying taxes on the borrowed gains (taxes may be required if policy is surrendered). As long as the policy stays in force the borrowed funds do not need to be repaid, but interest may be charged to your cash value account. Premiums are adjustable by the policy owner.

variable universal life insurance   A Variable Life insurance policy provides both a death benefit and an investment component called a cash value. The owner of the policy invests the cash value in subaccounts selected by the insurer. The policyholder may accumulate significant cash value over the years and "borrow" the appreciated funds without paying taxes on the borrowed gains (taxes may be required if policy is surrendered). As long as the policy stays in force the borrowed funds do not need to be repaid, but interest may be charged to your cash value account.

vesting   The law requires that a qualified plan have a schedule under which a participant earns an ownership interest in employer provided contributions based on his or her years of service with the employer. Amounts contributed by the participant are always 100% vested.

viatical settlement   Occurs when a person with terminal or chronic illness sells his/her life insurance policy to a third party for an amount that is less than the full amount of the death benefit. The buyer becomes the new owner and/or beneficiary of the life insurance policy, pays all future premiums, and collects the entire death benefit when the insured dies. Some states regulate the purchase as a security while others may regulate it as insurance.

waiver of premium   A waiver of premium rider on an insurance policy sets for conditions under which premium payments are not required to be made for a time. The most popular waiver of premium rider is the disability waiver under which the owner of the policy (also called the policyholder) is not required to make premium payments during a period of total disability.

whole life insurance   A traditional Whole Life insurance policy provides both a death benefit and a cash value component. The policy is designed to remain in force for a lifetime. Premiums stay level and the death benefit is guaranteed. Over time, the cash value of the policy grows and helps keep the premium level. Although the premiums start out significantly higher than that of a comparable term life policy, over time the level premium eventually is overtaken by the ever-increasing premium of a term policy.

will   The most basic and necessary of estate planning tools, a will is a legal document declaring a person's wishes regarding the disposition of their estate. A will ensures that the right people receive the right assets at the right time. If an individual dies without a will they are said to have died intestate.

wrap account   An account offered by investment dealers whereby investors are charged an annual management fee based on the value of invested assets.

yield   The yield on an investment is the total proceeds paid from the investment and is calculated as a percentage of the amount invested.

zero-coupon bond   A zero-coupon bond is a bond sold without interest-paying coupons. Instead of paying periodic interest, the bond is sold at a discount and pays its entire face amount upon maturity, which is usually a one year period or longer.

Endnotes

Chapter 1

[1] Investments compared to CDs and T-Bills are not insured while CDs are FDIC insured and the federal government guarantees T-bills. Nothing herein is intended to be legal or tax advice. Readers are encouraged to consult their accountant or attorney. Mention of a particular investment should not be considered a recommendation. Recommendations can only be made by determining your suitability. Past performance is not a guarantee of future results. Any rates quoted herein are subject to change. The S&P 500 and Dow Jones Industrial Averages are weighted, unmanaged indexes. Mutual fund performance figures are from Morningstar Principia as of 6/30/98. Stock market measurements are taken from Ibbotson and Associates 1997 Yearbook. Performance measurements of the Dow 5, 10, Fair Value portfolio and mutual funds are as of December 31, 1997 (unless otherwise stated) and include reinvested dividends and are before deductions for management fees or transaction costs.

Chapter 2

[2] http://www.bankrate.com
[3] Helen Huntley, "Callable CD sales draw inquiry from SEC officials," *St.* Petersburg Times, 12/29/00.
[4] *"Callable, bump-up, and step-up CDs,"* www.bankrate.com, 8/5/02.
[5] LaSalle Bank NA term sheet for a Callable S&P 500 Linked Certificate of Deposit, 7.5 Year Final Maturity, Non-Callable 2 Years dated 01/04.
[6] http://www.rmaarp.com/estimates.htm

Chapter 3

[7] "Speech by SEC Commissioner: *Mutual Fund Performance Advertising: Is It In Overdrive*? Remarks by Commissioner Paul R. Carey, U.S. Securities & Exchange Commission, at SEC Speaks, 3/2/01

[8] Russel Kinnel, *"The Truth About One Year Returns,"* 8/7/03 http://news.morningstar.com/doc/article/0,1,94882,00.html

[9] Morningstar Principia Pro Commentary, *Buying Unloved Funds*, 2/21/01.

[10] Buying Unloved Funds Could Yield Lovable Returns, by Gabriel Presler, 1/19/01.

[11] "The common stock of smaller companies may offer more potential for growth," www.wisi.com/mf1a.htm

[12] Former Vanguard Chairman and CEO John Bogle defines mean reversion this way: "In the world of investing, the mean is the powerful magnet that pulls market returns toward it, causing market returns to deteriorate after they exceed historical norms by subsequent margins and to improve after they fall short." http://mutualinvestor.com/smartinvestor/realisticexpectations.asp

[13] Putting Risk in its Place, John Rekenthaler Morningstar editorial 5/27/94. In the study, risk was defined as standard deviation

[14] Of 15,986 funds in the Morningstar Principia database as of 12/31/03, 210 funds had expense ratios of 3% or more and 142 had expense ratios of 1/10th of 1% or less.

[15] Morningstar Principia Pro, 12/31/03.

[16] Stefan Sharkansky, *Mutual Funds Costs: Risk Without Reward*, 5/02.

[17] Ibid.

[18] Source: CDA/Wiesenberger 1983-1996, press release 12/01/1997 from web site, Barrons 1997 and 1998, "Fund Managers Get Rich, But Not Their Customers" 12/29/1997, Morningstar Principia database, 12/31/1999. Past performance does not guarantee future results. No investment strategy can guarantee protection from losses. This table assumes reinvestment of dividends at year-end. The above results are hypothetical and do not take into account any commissions, taxes and expenses. The S&P 500 and the Dow Jones Industrial Averages are unmanaged indexes. It is possible to invest in an index. The index does not take into consideration expenses, fees or commissions.

Chapter 4

[19] Assumes a combined rate of 28% federal and 5% state which applies to single filers earning $70,350 and married filing jointly earning $117,250 in 2004.

[20] 17 years, the life expectancy of a 70 year old. The actual results will vary depending on actual lifetime, actual health rating, actual tax rates and earnings on the IRA.

[21] Calculated by growing the balance each year by a hypothetical 10% and distributing the required minimum distributions per IRS Publication 590

[22] This income tax may not be payable all at once as proper beneficiary designations may allow the tax to be paid over the life of the beneficiaries.

[23] Estate tax based on total estate of $2,315,720. Estate tax on Income in Respect of a Decedent can be recovered by the heirs.

[24] The purchase of life insurance may involve significant expenses, fees and surrender charges. Not everyone can qualify for life insurance and such qualification and rate is based on health. If the policy is deemed to be a modified endowment contract, distributions of earnings are taxable.

[25] First Penn Pacific Titan One, current interest rate of 5.5%, continuous annual payments of $12,980 based on non-smoker preferred rating provides a death benefit of $500,000 free of estate and income tax if properly purchased and owned outside the insured's estate. 3/9/04

[26] This technique may not be beneficial in every situation.

[27] IRS Publication 590

[28] Natalie B. Choate, *Life and Death Planning for Retirement Benefits*, Fifth Edition, 2003.

[29] Private Letter Ruling 2001-26041.

[30] The cost of establishing an IRA trust or IRA asset will varies by location and attorney and may be significant.

[31] Assumes a combined rate of 28% federal and 5% state which applied to single filers earning $70,350 and married filing jointly earning $117,250 in 2004. The value of the IRA is not a factor.

[32] Income tax of 33% plus estate tax of 48% on the after tax amount: .33 + .48 (1-.33) = 65% tax.

[33] The average turnover of stocks categorized as "domestic stock funds" was 124% in 2003. Data from Morningstar Principia Pro, 12/31/03.

[34] http://www.irs.gov/pub/irs-news/ir02-104.pdf

[35] http://www.irahelp.com/pr_100302.shtml
[36] **http://www.ncee.net/summit/**
2002SummitExecutiveSummary.pdf
[37] *The Wall Street Journal*, October 9, 2002

Chapter 5

[38] 1997 Society of Actuaries Nursing Home Survey
[39] Most states have a $2,000 cap on assets, but a few go up to $4,000 and some go as low as $1,000. Average for all states is $2,146 as of 01/21/04.   http://www.ltcconsultants.com/consumer/wyslyk/index.shtml
[40] California Advocates for Nursing Home Reform
[41] Technical Report 1-01, Scripps Gerontology Center, Feb. 2001
[42] A 2002 survey of 2,462 skilled and intermediate care nursing homes in all 50 states conducted by General Electric Capital Assurance Company found monthly costs ranging from $3,000 to $12,475 with an average cost of $4,698.
[43] Most states have a $2,000 cap on assets, but a few go up to $4,000 and some go as low as $1,000. Average for all states is $2,146 as of 01/21/04.   http://www.ltcconsultants.com/consumer/wyslyk/index.shtml
[44] *Taking Care of Tomorrow: A Consumer's Guide to Long-Term Care*, California Department of Aging
[45] *Avoid Fraud When Buying Long-Term Care Insurance: A Guide For Consumers And Their Families*, Richard Alexander, editor, p. 8.
[46] As an example, life investors, married, preferred base plan, 1,500 day coverage, 5% compounded inflation, 90-day elimination for nursing home, 0 days for homecare. Annual costs rise as follows: Age 60: $1,120.11, Age 65: $1,376.60, Age 70: $1,849.40, Age 75: $2,684.60, rates as of 3/12/04.
[47] Source: Federal LTC Insurance Program Brochure, Jan. 2004
[48] Lincoln Benefit Life Policy Form LB-6301-P-Q, nursing home only, 5 years coverage, 90 day elimination period, preferred health rating and an initial daily benefit of $110 per day with 5% compounded inflation for a California resident. Total benefit assumes start of 5 year stay in 2030, rates quoted 1/21/04.
[49] General Electric Financial, Long-Term Care overview.
[50] "Both men and women said providing care affected their family lives, but more women cited this effect, 73 percent compared to 60 percent. And more than twice as many women than men said

providing long-term care assistance had a significant impact on their own health, 40 percent compared to 18 percent. Fifty-six percent of female respondents described long-term care as a "very big problem" compared to 42 percent of male respondents." *Elder Life Planning News*, Volume 1, Issue 2.

[51] In the Middle: A Report on Multicultural Boomers Coping With Family and Aging Issues, July 2001.

[52] Technical Report 1-01, Scripps Gerontology Center, Feb 2001 found that 14.6% of residents required a nursing home stay of 5 years or more.

[53] Ibid.

[54] A 2002 survey of 2,462 skilled and intermediate care nursing homes in all 50 states conducted by General Electric Capital Assurance Company found an average monthly cost of $4,698.

[55] Technical Report 1-01, Scripps Gerontology Center, Feb. 2001 found that 28% of people required a nursing home stay of more than 3 years.

[56] A 2002 survey of 2,462 skilled and intermediate care nursing homes in all 50 states conducted by General Electric Capital Assurance Company found an average daily rate of approximately $155/day.

[57] If you have sufficient interest income or Social Security income, it may be better for you to insure for a majority of the cost of long-term care and self-insure for the remainder. This has the effect of lowering the current cost of the insurance premiums without subjecting you to being unable to cover the costs of long-term care, if and when they arise.

[58] Average hourly rate, MetLife Market Survey of Nursing Home and Home Care Costs, August 2003.

[59] 65-year-old, nonsmoking female in good health. Lincoln National Policy Form LL-2020 series, 01/04, single premium fixed UL policy includes a long-term care benefit rider and a return of principal feature provided no loans or withdrawals are taken. Four percent minimum interest rate, death benefit guaranteed to age 100. Benefits and guarantee based on the claims-paying ability of the insurer. There are no minimum interest rates required to keep the death benefit or long-term care benefit in force for the policyholder's life, provided there are no loans or withdrawals. Minimum required single premium is $10,000. This policy is a modified endowment contract and loans or withdrawals of account value in excess of premiums paid are taxed as ordinary income. The purchase of life insurance and long-term care insurance requires a health review and not everyone is insurable.

The purchase of insurance incurs fees, expenses, and commissions and possible surrender charges.

[60] 1035 exchange

[61] Based on the claims paying ability of the insurance company

[62] Technical Report 1-01, Scripps Gerontology Center, Feb. 2001.

[63] Ibid

[64] Ibid

[65] http://www.kiplinger.com/retreport/archives/2000/June/manage.htm

[66] WSJ 08/05/03 Metlife survey

Chapter 7

[67] CDs are FDIC insured while annuities and municipal bonds are not. Municipal bonds are guaranteed by the issuing authority and annuity guarantees are subject to the claims-paying ability of the insurance company. Municipal bond interest is free of federal tax (and may also be free of state tax) and may be subject to alternative minimum tax. Annuity interest is taxed upon withdrawal and withdrawals prior to age 59½ are subject to 10% penalty. Taxes are assumed at 33% (combined federal tax rate of 28% and state tax rate of 5%).

[68] From the taxable alternative, you remove money each year to pay taxes (taxes assumed at 33%—a combined 28% federal and 5% state tax rate

[69] the average interest rate being paid on a single-premium deferred annuity based on the top 100 annuities as reported by Comparative Annuity Reports 1/04

[70] Withdrawals prior to age 59½ incur a 10% penalty. Withdrawals are taxed as ordinary income of interest.

[71] Monthly payments are based on the claims-paying ability of the insurer, so picking a financially solid insurance company is important. Immediate annuity payments may incur premium taxes in some states and will contain fees and expenses.

[72] The exclusion ratio is described in IRS Publication 17, 2003. Each payment is comprised of principal and interest. This is an average of fixed immediate annuity payments from the top 40 annuity companies as reported by Comparative Annuity Reports as of January 2004, male, age 75, lifetime monthly payments. Lifetime payment guarantee is based on the claims-paying ability of the insurance company. Each insurance company may use a different assumption as to life

expectancy and assumed interest rate in calculating their annuity payments. These assumptions are not publicly disclosed. Immediate annuities may not be surrendered.

[73] Each immediate annuity payment is comprised of interest and principal as determined by actuarial calculations. The principal portion is not taxable. Once the entire premium has been recovered through principal payments, the remaining payments are fully taxed as ordinary income. The purchase of municipal bonds incurs a commission. The purchase of annuities incurs commissions, fees, and potential surrender charges. Municipal bonds may be subject to alternative minimum tax.

[74] Rate on 15 year, AAA rated municipal bonds, Bloomberg, 3/10/04. Fifteen-year bonds closely approximate Mr. Jones' 16-year life expectancy to provide a sound basis for comparison with a lifetime immediate annuity expected to pay for 16 years as of 3/10/04.

[75] Based on the average payout for the top 40 single-premium deferred annuities as reported by Comparative Annuity Reports, 01/04.

[76] the tax-free portion of an immediate annuity is the part the IRS considers return of your principal and is based on your life expectancy and the expected return

[77] Combined federal and state tax rate of 33% accounting for 74% exclusion. The exclusion is the percentage of principal returned to total payments. Total anticipated payments for 16-year life expectancy (IRS Publication 590) are $672,960 making 74% of payments non-taxable ($500,000 original premium/$672,960 total payments).

[78] Premiums for immediate annuities include commissions, fees and potential surrender charges.

[79] There is also a tax benefit exclusive to annuities when annuitized. Of each payment, the IRS considers a part of your periodic payments return of your original investment, which is not taxed, and part is your gain, taxed at ordinary rates. Note that withdrawals prior to age 59½ are subject to a 10% IRS penalty. Variable annuities have mortality, expense and surrender charges and mutual funds may have redemption costs. Variable annuities have a death benefit. Withdrawals of interest are taxed as ordinary income. This is not a comprehensive discussion of tax issues and you should consult a tax advisor.

[80] Different insurance companies offer different benefits. There is an additional cost for these features and are guaranteed by the claims paying ability of the insurer. Both return and principal value of mutual funds and variable annuities will fluctuate, and they may be worth more or less than their original costs when redeemed. Variable

annuities and mutual funds involve investment risk, including possible loss of principal. Withdrawals and under-performance of its subaccounts will have the effect of decreasing cash values and the death benefit. Withdrawals in excess of the cost basis will be taxable. Variable annuities and mutual funds are sold by prospectus, which contains more complete information including risk factors, fees, surrender charges and other costs. You should obtain a prospectus from your financial representative. Please read the prospectuses carefully before you make a purchase or invest.

[81] Methods of calculating interest vary between annuities as do minimum and maximum interest rates, so read the brochure or policy carefully. Subject to the claims-paying ability of the insurer, which is not government guaranteed. You can also lose principal by taking loans or early withdrawals from the annuity, or due to other fees and charges. Gains may only be vested at the end of the annuity term and withdrawals may seriously erode total return. Additionally, annual withdrawals are typically limited to 10% annually or surrender charges apply. The principal guarantee of index annuities applies to annuities held to term. **If liquidated prior to term, policyholders can lose money.** The level of principal protection varies by annuity, so read any brochure and policy carefully to determine what charges and risk to principal exist.

[82] CDs are FDIC insured while annuities are not. Annuities are guaranteed by the claims-paying ability of the insurer.

[83] Deferred Annuity price trends from www.annuityshopper.com 1988 show average rates for single premium deferred annuities of 9.4% and Comparative Annuity Reports January 2004 show average rates of 3.72%. Exchanging annuities may incur surrender charges and a new schedule of surrender charges, fees and expenses. Before exchanging an annuity, consider any remaining surrender charges from your existing annuity and that you may have a new schedule of surrender charges in the new annuity.

[84] IRS Publication 709, 2004.

[85] Variable Life Insurance is sold by prospectus that will be provided by your financial representative. Please consider investment objectives, risks, charges, and expenses before investing. For this and other information about any variable annuity and its underlying investments, please call the variable annuity provider to request a prospectus. Please read it carefully before you invest. Both return and principal value of the portfolios in the policy will fluctuate, and the portfolios may be worth more or less than their original costs when redeemed.

Variable products involve investment risk, including possible loss of principal. Withdrawals, policy loans, and under-performance of its subaccounts will have the effect of decreasing cash values and the death benefit. Withdrawals in excess of the cost basis will be taxable.

[86] When you exchange real estate, you do not actually exchange one property for another. You sell your property and those funds go immediately into escrow for the new property you are purchasing. Such an exchange is tax free.

[87] You select a rate based on IRS limits, lifetime annual income and have the property out of your hair and out of your estate (and at the same time create a nice donation for your favorite charities when you pass on and a nice tax deduction for yourself.

Chapter 8

[88] Generation skipping tax could apply.

[89] **Not all inherited assets qualify for the current step-up in basis capital gains tax break.**

[90] http://www.cfpa.org/issues/estatetax/index.cfm

[91] The only way to escape the transfer for value rule is if you and your child are business partners.

Testimonials

"Financial planning is one of those areas I had always intended on doing something about but never really got around to it. The fact of the matter is, between dealing with tenant concerns, updating properties, searching for new properties and spending time with my family, my finances always seemed to take a back seat. Now, I'd done some things in the past to address my financial situation. Still, somewhere in the back of mind I worried what would happen to my family if I wasn't around to manage the properties? What if someone slipped and fell? Were my properties generating enough income? Could I be doing better? How much longer did I want to be a landlord? Would I ever officially retire? I had remembered reading a financial column in the MRHA newsletter written by Marcus Papajohn. Not sure exactly what to expect, I gave him a call.

Marcus Papajohn is my financial planner. He answers my questions and concerns in a very comfortable and straightforward way. Marcus has helped me better understand my business and has provided me with a direction and a focus that I didn't have before. I now understand what I can expect from my business in the future. In working together with my CPA, Estate Attorney and real estate brokers, Marcus has shown me how to better utilize other resources available to me. I can't promise you'll like everything Marcus has to tell you, but sometimes the truth stings a little bit before you make things better."

–David Heroux, Fall River, MA

"I have worked with a number of different financial planners over the years and Marcus is the first person to explain things to me in a language I can easily understand."

–Patricia Thomas, Hanson, MA

"After years of saving toward retirement, we needed just the right person to help us plan for the future. Marcus has been the perfect fit for us. In his professional yet friendly manner, he has guided us toward the path we want to be on. He has helped us organize, given suggestions, and answered all our questions. We would recommend him to others in need of guidance in senior financial planning."

–Ronald & Mary Piccuito, Marshfield, MA

"Our investments had been stagnating because we didn't know who to trust and didn't feel that we could manage them ourselves. Marcus has been a patient and knowledgeable resource for us. Marcus has tailored things to our needs and time frame. It has been a great relief to find someone with his honesty and experience."

–Paul & Ellen Dean, Foxboro, MA

"When we need to bounce an idea off of someone we go to Marcus first. He helps us to remove ourselves from the situation and to see all of the different angles and to keep us on the right track."

–James & Lynn Ayers , Fitchburg, MA

"Marcus Papajohn is upfront and honest with me about my finances. He tells me what I need to know when I want to know it without having to call him 25 times for an answer. He keeps things simple and easy to understand and that is gratifying to me."

–Valerie Teague, Lakeville, MA

Biography

Marcus A. Papajohn is recognized as a leading financial expert in the Boston area. His practice concentrates on helping those who want to protect their principal and insure that their money lasts. Mr. Papajohn has assisted over 500 people to lower their taxes, in some cases by as much as 50%, reduce taxes on social security income, limit estate taxes, and protect their estate values. He is also a member of the Society of Certified Senior Advisors (SCSA) – and is one of only 11,000 people in the country to have completed a 17 part program on the study of senior and retirement issues. He and his wife Sarah reside in the South Shore area of Massachusetts.